Lessons of the Heart

Celebrating the Rhythms of Life

Lessons of the Heart

PATRICIA H. LIVINGSTON

FOREWORD BY HENRI NOUWEN

AVE MARIA PRESS Notre Dame, Indiana 46556

Patricia Livingston, a respected counsellor and featured speaker at retreats, workshops and seminars, is Associate Director of the Center for Continuing Formation in Ministry at the University of Notre Dame. *Lessons of the Heart* is her first book. Her audio tapes include *The Hunger and The Feast, Learning from Life,* and *Made for Union, Meant for Love* (all from Ave Maria Press). Her numerous articles and interviews have appeared in *Praying, St. Anthony Messenger,* and *Studies in Formative Spirituality,* and she received the 1990 *U.S. Catholic* Award for significant contribution to the cause of women in the church.

First printing, August, 1992
Fourth printing, August, 1996
27,000 copies in print

Acknowledgment:

Chapter 4,"Spirituality Is *Not* Removed From Life" appeared in a slightly different form in *Praying* magazine under the title, "Over The Pudding and Under The Hairdryer."

International Standard Book Number: 0-87793-486-X

Library of Congress Catalog Card Number: 92-72924

Cover and text design by Elizabeth J. French

Printed and bound in the United States of America.

Dedication

To my children
"special, fragile, unrepeatable"
each with an arresting freshness
utterly different from the others
this book is for you.
I hope you do not understand it all yet.
The day will come.
I wish with part of me that it would not.
But it will.
You cannot live into the fullness of your life without
the complex interplay of light and dark.
And if you could, it would not match the stature of
your hearts.
So,
when there comes a time that angst moves in, a
claxon shrills, the world falls dark;
or when you puzzle up against the border of what
you understand
and find yourself groping for the truth of what life is,
read this again.
It is the best that I can tell you for those times.
The brief of it is this:
Love is stronger than pain.
Laughter has more power even than death.
And most of all . . .
God loves.
God loves.
All you know of loving
shows you God.

Contents

Foreword

The beauty of *Lessons of the Heart* is that it makes little things shine brightly. Our lives consist of many little things: little events, little tasks, little encounters, little surprises. Although we read often in the newspapers about spectacular happenings and watch great dramas on TV, our own daily life seems mostly ordinary.

But is it ordinary, or do we lack the eyes to see the mystery hidden in the ordinary?

Pat Livingston gives us eyes for the hidden treasures of our lives. She helps us to see that something divine is present in the human, that something hopeful is happening in our usual ways, that an aspect of love shines through our hidden behavior, and that a divine gift is buried right at our feet.

Through many stories, anecdotes, and observations, Pat Livingston helps us to discover and celebrate the sacred in the mundane, or, to say it more theologically, to discover and celebrate the sacramentality of our existence.

As I read this book, I often said to myself, "Oh, I also can tell simple stories like that!" But every time I said this to myself, I felt invited to realize that my little stories were, in fact, part of a much greater story—the story of God's active presence in my life.

Lessons of the Heart is a truly hopeful book, a book that opens our eyes to see the mystery of God right where we are.

HENRI J. M. NOUWEN

1

Truths for Claiming Life

Years ago I drove a hundred miles each way for every class of a master's program. How I got through those endless stretches of central Florida backland--early in the morning and very late at night--I'm not certain today.

But I remember what helped me the most.

When I would wear out the radio (stations would just fuzz out after a while, and it was long before tape decks), when I would give up on singing things or trying to gather ideas for my next paper due that term, I would memorize. I would bring poetry and passages from plays and books. In the dashboard light I would glance at lines and say them over and over until I knew them.

My favorite was from Shakespeare. After all these years, I remember it still: King Henry V's speech to his troops the night before the battle of Agincourt. Most of the other things I learned are gone. The e.e. cummings was too intricate to retain without on-going practice. I have only phrases of Hopkins and Dickinson; some paragraphs of *The Little Prince.*

But I have Henry's speech. The English have come to fight the French and only realize as darkness falls and they see the enemy campfires, that they are outnumbered five to one. It is a speech for courage, a call to heart and hope, a pouring out of the power to trust and bond and not retreat. It is the eve before St. Crispin's Feast, and King Hal predicts about that feast that "From this day until the ending of the world, . . . we, in it, will be remembered. We few, we happy few, we band of brothers" (Act IV, Scene iii).

I would say this speech over and over to myself on those dark roads, trying to rally my own courage and trust, reliving the fact that those English troops did not run, that against all odds they were somehow able to stand and win. One line moved me every time: "This story shall the good man teach his son."

I feel that way about the stories in this book. They are stories to tell, to teach each other, stories for women and for men; for the daughter and son in all of us who go to battle now. Not to actual war (we pray and work that this will not continue to be seen as a solution), not against the French, but against all the overwhelming forces of the night.

I write this book to gather things I have spoken to myself and offered in my work. They have been for me truths for claiming life. They are distillations of happenings that can help against both fears and losses, mortal hurts and nagging "but, what ifs?" They are for the parts of us that hear the phone call in the middle of the night, or know the mutiny at the core of confidence when rejection sends us sprawling on the pavement of our world. They are for the parts of us that remember the awkwardness of growing up and that begin to know the gradual erosion of growing old. They are what I have come to call lessons of the heart.

We are more aware of them sometimes than others. For me awareness often happens when I come home. Most of the year now I am an associate director of a sabbatical program—an updating, renewal program for men and women in full-time ministry in the Catholic church. It is called the Center for Continuing Formation in Ministry and is sponsored by the University of Notre Dame. The program has been offered since 1976, and I had taught in it every spring and fall for ten years before I took this job. I have a nine-month contract which allows me to come back to Florida for Christmas and summers to the house where my children grew up. It is summer now and I am home.

I feel flooded with meaning here, very aware of the passage of time. Partly it is because of all the memories. I see the corner where we put the Christmas tree, the places, like inside the clock, where Easter eggs were always hidden. I reach for a pan to heat some soup, and it brings back all those meals: eggs and grits, creamed chipped beef, tacos every Friday night.

I open up a door to get the dust pan to brush up crumbs I spilled, and there they are, the measurements on the broom closet door. Marked in columns one by one for the three children, edging up: Kadee, Randy, Boo. The oldest is now the shortest, the youngest the most tall. (Lots of hassle and delight surrounded that reversal.)

So many traces of their growing up are in this house. Taking a message yesterday, I reached into the kitchen drawer and only later did I see that the pencil I picked up was stamped with the name of the grade school where they went. It must have once been in someone's pencil box, carried with a lunch pail, waiting for a bus. Fred Wild School. "That Fred, he sure was Wild" they used to say, and crack up laughing.

Meaning seems to come with the passage of time. We are aware of it at homecomings. It also happens at big events. Rituals. Ceremonies. Boo (whose real name is Robert Edward) just graduated from college. He was commissioned into the Army the same day. I pinned on one of his gold Lieutenant's bars, the young woman that he loves pinning on the other.

He looked at me and grinned, a grin much like his father's. Suddenly I realized that exactly thirty years before, his father had graduated from West Point. I had pinned a bar on him, *his* mother on the other side. As I remembered, I was struck. Thirty years! Thirty years! Where did they go? This handsome laughing man before me fully grown, and he the youngest, the little one, the last one born, now *grown*.

"Life is like a moving walkway," someone said to me this spring. We are all on it, moving with the same pace of days, leaving the years behind.

The line advances. When I was a child, my father was in the Army. Then, at twenty, I was an Army wife. Now the Army means my children: Boo newly commissioned; Randy just released, home from war in the Persian Gulf.

I was struck by how the walkway moves us up in generations when I opened the paper on Sunday and there was a feature in the entertainment section about Superman. A new rendition titled *Superboy* is being made, and the actors who originally played Jimmy Olsen and Lois Lane are back with parts in the new movie.

Their picture stunned me. I remember them as the young reporters on *The Daily Planet*. Here they were, forty years later, sitting together, touching hands, delightful smiles turned to us. But grandparents! Lois and Jimmy! Gray haired and lined, age spots on both their hands, they were evidence of how the walkway moves all of us on. Only Superman remains the same.

Three years ago last summer I was invited to a wedding reception. The actual wedding was up north, but the bride and groom dressed up again to give a party here. I remember the groom when he was ten, the skinniest kid in elementary school. He was all angles and planes, not a single curve. His ears stuck out, and he had a permanently startled look in his big eyes. Now here he stood, smiling, proud, his arm around a dark-haired wife in long white lace. Still very tall, his body had filled out. The planes and angles in his face had somehow grown into handsome, his hair a little long, covering up his ears. He looked at her and kissed her very gently.

Beside him stood my Randy—blonde, brawny, joking; teeth white in his face browned from working in the orange groves. When did he start looking like a man and not a boy?

When did these two, who had been in scrapes I hate to think about, become adult? When did the brash wear off? Where was the ultra-cool discarded?

Across the grass came a young woman with a baby. I recognized her suddenly--a classmate of theirs. A baby! Giggling, showing off a tooth, square and sharp. They were all like that not long ago. It *wasn't* long ago. The laugh that crinkled up their eyes and made their noses turn up. We held them on our hips in just that way. The moving walkway.

I have a nephew named Sam, my younger sister's child. He is a marvelous character with ten creative ideas before he gets to breakfast. He likes the notion of moving around in time. Once I forgot his birthday until the very day, and I called to tell him he would have to have a time warp when the package came, go back to this day, to his birthday, when he opened it. He loved that. Time warping ten days later was more fun than the presents I picked out.

In our imagination (Sam's and mine at least) we move around with ease. But in our lives, we don't. We have to continue on the walkway in the same square that is ours since birth. We cannot alter the pace of days.

I was witness years ago to the first moment of realization of the inexorable advancing of time--and a brilliant attempt to dodge out of it--on the part of Megan, the daughter of my dear friend Mary. Megan sucked her thumb. She had gravely agreed that when she had her fourth birthday, she would not suck her thumb anymore. The morning after her fourth birthday party, her mom saw her sitting propped up on her pillows with her thumb in her mouth. "What's this?" her mom asked. Meg pulled out her thumb and held it up, observing it. "This," she said matter-of-factly, "is a three-year-old thumb in a four-year-old mouth."

Years ago when my oldest was only ten months old, my husband went to law school. It was in Gainesville, an old Florida town. There was a woman I used to see when I would push the stroller over the brick sidewalks. She was always wearing black, and holding an open black umbrella as a parasol. She had beautiful posture and a very private expression on her face. Her hair was long and white, twisted up on her head. The students used to call her "Arsenic and Old Lace," and the rumor was that her husband had been a very famous admiral and had died in war. I would see her from time to time in every quarter of the town. She must have walked miles.

One day when I was hanging diapers out for both the children (by then Randy had been born, joining Kadee in the nursery) I was distracted from the pins and clothes on my own line. Stretching across the back of the apartment next to ours were six black dresses hanging in a row. Six black dresses. I had never known who lived in the apartment on the other side of our nursery wall. I had never heard a sound beyond a small, dry cough, so faint it might have been the wind.

With all the noise that filled our place—the crying of a newborn in the night, the creak of rockers, the tantrums of a two-year-old—I had hardly given it much thought. Looking at the dresses, like huge blackbirds turned upside down on the line, it came to me with force. The admiral's wife—Arsenic and Old Lace whom I'd been seeing and admiring in her peculiar dignity since I had come here—lived next door.

I never saw her laundry out again. I never saw her go out through the door. But all these years I've had that image deeply held. It strikes me for us all. On the other side of the nursery wall for all of us there is our own old age, the frailty, eccentricity, and wisdom of our final time.

My mother has an image of a diving board. "I feel as if I've climbed the ladder of the high dive," she explains, "and it is almost my turn to jump off. I'm scared to jump. I turn around to climb back down, but I can't. All the other people are there in line. I will have to go off into the deep. I think it will be good. The dive has always been worth it. But I can't help being scared."

The passage of time. In the process of all those days and nights and endless afternoons we meet with life. And in that interchange, sometimes grappling, sometimes dancing, we come upon meaning. It doesn't happen all at once. We glimpse it first, and gradually it deepens, the way a day grows light.

I have a friend who used to get up with me on New Year's Day and go into the woods to watch the new year dawn. Sometimes her husband would drive us in his jeep to find a spot, would stomp around to drive off snakes, would search carefully for nests of fire ants. We would find a place as restful as we could, and then we'd wait. It happens very slowly, a lessening of dark. You know it when there begins to be silhouettes of things against the sky. Next you notice some shape. Dimension comes; texture. Then there are shades of gray, tinges less than black. Very slowly color comes. Greens begin, and browns, and the rose-ing of the sky.

Meaning is like that for me. It happens gradually. Often I can't distinguish it at first, but then a silhouette may form, and texture shows itself; then growing grays, then color coming full. It happens in the passages of time. Only life can teach us truth. Revelation happens in experience. Day to day we learn the lessons of the heart.

2

Life Is Mixed

One of the most important learnings for me is that life is mixed. When I say it now, it sounds totally obvious, but the centrality of the truth of the mixedness of life took a long time to fully dawn in me. Slowly I grasped that life is filled with contrasts, with seasons, with alternating rhythms, cadences, and forms. In every sense it is an interplay of light and dark. Polarities and paradox, creative tension between opposites, form the living-out of our being.

Carl Jung describes this with great power, but it was ancient wisdom long before. Madeleine L'Engle observed "It's said that the greatest single thing the Greeks contributed to civilization was giving us 'on the one hand' and 'on the other hand.'"[1] Life is hardly ever just one or just the other. It is a tension involved in the complexity of both/and. Tevye in *Fiddler on the Roof* sings this struggle in a way we recognize as truth.

There are a thousand forms of mixedness, they will appear throughout this book. We fight knowing it. We want life to be all good. We rail against the times things do not work, against the scrapes and disappointments, the mistakes and letdowns. There is an outrage that we feel: "This shouldn't be!" we cry, and feel ill-used.[2]

Crying out does not help. The struggle and rejecting of what happens makes the burden more. (I always struggle first, however. It never happens smoothly that I say "Oh, good, here is the mix of life again! A chance to grow. . . .") As hard as it is, that our life is mixed is a precious thing to learn. To recognize it as a thing like winter, and accept, trying not to prolong the "This should not be!"

When I was first beginning to face this mix myself, it was confirmed for me by a stranger in a check-out line.

I was in a rather primitive grocery store on the outskirts of where I live in central Florida. It was one of those stores that will never have a computer cash register, and where the peanut butter cheese crackers are lined up by the counter with the beef jerky and the chewing tobacco. It was a store where there was a definite layer of dirt on the cleaning materials. It might remind you of the store in Lake Wobegon in Garrison Keilor's "Prairie Home Companion" that he calls Ralph's Pretty Good Grocery. Ralph's motto is "If we don't have it, you can probably get along without it."

The woman behind me in line was black. She was about my age, but she looked older. She was heavy and tall and weary looking, leaning on the handle of the grocery basket as if to take pressure off feet that had hurt her almost as long as she could remember. She gave a great sigh, totally unselfconsciously, sighing to herself.

"Are you O.K.?" I asked her as gently as I could.

"Sure," she said, "sure. But life is hard. It sure is hard. Yes Ma'am, it's hard." She was talking mostly to herself, like the sigh had been to herself.

Well, it is. That's part of the secret. My mom has a saying: "Life is just a bowl of cherries . . . with pits!"

My great-aunt told me on a Kentucky porch swing one summer afternoon when I was too young to understand: "There's no perfect situation, honey." And there's not.

But there is more to it. The woman in the grocery line turned to me, and after saying, more to herself than to me, that life was hard, she smiled. It was a wonderful smile. There was more irony in it than in all the plays of Molière. It was slow and wide, and it ended with her saying to me, straight and clear, as if it were very important that I know: "But life is good."

"It really is," I replied, and I meant that to both the hard and the good.

Then she said, "Did you get you some eggs? They cheap today. Half price."

"No, I didn't notice."

"Got to keep your eyes open, gal," she directed, "Go get you some. I'll save your place in line."

Reaching for my eggs I felt a gratitude begin that I've had to this day for her confirming what I'd known, but not quite said aloud 'til then.

There are lots of layers of learning things. We have to have experience before we can understand. Just having things happen to me didn't teach me. I have always had to reflect on what the meaning could be in the experience. "What did I learn?" I'd ask myself.

I did not realize this had become a habit. One morning when I was visiting my sister Peggy, her first-grade daughter, Margy, was having breakfast with me at six o'clock. (It had been her idea when I was sound asleep.) As we poured milk on our cereal she asked me in her clear, crisp voice, "Aunt Pat, what is your favorite sentence stem?"

"My favorite sentence stem, Marg?"

"You know what a sentence stem is, don't you, Aunt Pat? It is a series of sentences that all begin with the same phrase, but have different endings."

"Yes. I think I can almost remember what a sentence stem is, Margy. I guess it is just narrowing it down to my favorite right now that is giving me trouble."

"I have been listening to you and my mom talk, and I think I know what your favorite sentence stem is."

"Well, let me hear it, Marg."

"I think your favorite sentence stem is: 'The learning from that is . . . (dot . . . dot . . . dot).'"

She was right! Looking at her lovely bright face over the blue bowl of Cheerios, I was amazed. She's right! "What did I learn?" I try to ask that of myself again and again. Then attempt to answer "The learning from that is . . . ."

A major learning, confirmed by the woman in the grocery store, is that life is mixed, both hard and good. The truth of this was very strong one baseball season years ago. Both boys were playing Little League. They were on *different* teams, which meant I lived at that field, with twice-weekly games and driving back and forth to practices for each of them. I could have had my address changed to the ballpark that season.

Randy is the older son. He has a kind of dynamism, a star aura. When he was born, after a prolonged and complicated labor and delivery, the doctor held him up. He had eye contact with me and the assembled medical personnel, and smiled. I said to the nurse, "If I didn't know better, I would say the baby smiled."

"Lady," she said, "I've worked in this delivery room for twenty years: he did, the baby smiled."

So he was born smiling. And he has kept up the aura of a star being born ever since. The problem is that this mystique puts a lot of pressure on him to perform.

When he played Little League Baseball, he had been playing two years and had never had a good hit. It was amazing how the stands were filled with hopeful fans who knew his moment must be coming.

One night it came. On the first pitch over the plate he swung and hit it: CRACK! Over the fence!

He took off running: first base, second, third . . . rounding third he took his hat off and bowed to the fans who had always known that it was only a matter of time. They were on their feet, yelling rebel yells.

As he crossed the plate, the umpire said, "Son, you're out. You threw your bat."

Now I don't mean to sound defensive, but this was a shock. He was a substitute umpire from the higher levels of Little League. Bat throwing was not a rule that these kids had been drilled on much. Barely heard of might describe it.Two innings later Randy was up again. The same thing happened. The first pitch: CRACK! Over the fence. He took off running. The umpire took off after him. He caught him by his jersey near first base.

"Son, look at your bat! You're OUT."

In his euphoria that he had pulled it off yet another time, Randy had really let the bat go. It was near third base.

I was behind the cage at home plate. I had been on concession stand duty. It is some kind of rule of life that when your kid gets a hit, you're probably selling hot dogs. I had come out to watch. The umpire's back was to me, but I could plainly see my Randy's face. All the color drained from it, which was when I discovered that rage is white and not red. I waited. I knew his vocabulary. I knew the air was about to turn blue over that ball field. I knew he would probably be banned from competitive sports in Highlands County forever. He jammed his hands down in his pockets. Thirty full long seconds went by. And then he said "Yes sir," and went to the dugout.

When the game was over (which they lost by two runs) I waited for him while he went through the ritual of shaking hands with the other team, getting a Coke, punching his teammates on the arms. When most of the people had cleared out I edged up to him.

"Randy, can I talk to you about the game?"

"I guess so, Mom."

"What you just experienced is a truth that is at the heart of life. What you know is something many people don't learn until they are much older. You have learned that *life is not fair.*

When the day finally comes that we hit the home run we've been waiting years for, we can be called out for some minor infraction of a rule we've barely heard of. And sometimes it happens not once, but twice. You also learned—and I'm so proud of you that the two home runs are nothing compared to it—that when this happens we must somehow face it and go on with dignity."

Scuffing his cleated tennis shoe in the red Florida clay, he said very low, "Momma, I think I learned that from you."

I was absolutely amazed. That was a moment I have really hung on to. I really wanted to needlepoint it and hang it on my kitchen wall.

A corollary happened a few weeks later. Boo, the youngest, was having his game. It was his second year playing for the same team, and the second year they put him on the bench for three quarters of the time, and then in the outfield for the tail end. The coach and his wife seemed to me to run the team like a setting for the diamond who was their son. The coach's wife was a Supermom, ex-Miss America type woman. When Boo came up to bat for the first time, she got up and went to the concession stand.

He had a batting technique. He was careful about swinging because he was short, and it was hard for those pitchers to throw a strike. Often if he just stood there, he could walk. Once he was on base he could run like the wind, saw every chance, and often made it home. This night the pitcher threw a pitch that hit the bat right above his hands. It dribbled off into the grass and Boo took off. The pitcher was so stunned, that by the time he picked it up, Boo slid around second base and never stopped. The pitcher overthrew at third and Boo came home.

The crowd went wild. The coach's wife came back.

"What happened?" she asked me.

I looked right into her Supermom, ex-Miss America face and said: "Boo hit a home run."

The flip side of *life is not fair* is that *sometimes we get incredible breaks in our favor.*

Life is mixed. Strangers say it in a check-out line. We learn it from our kids. We also see it in the arts. One of my favorite examples of this is from the movie *Little Big Man*. Dustin Hoffman plays a white man who turns into an Indian who turns into a white man then into an Indian depending on which side is winning in the current exchange. In the interludes when he is with the tribe he has a mentor, a magnificent character named Grandfather.

One day, when Hoffman and the other braves are gone from the camp, Custer's men raid, killing many women and children. When the men come back, Grandfather announces that he has lived long enough. "It is a good day to die," he says. He puts on his best buckskins and his huge feathered headdress and goes up the mountain to die. Hoffman goes with him. Grandfather gives a powerful speech to the Great Spirit, then lies down, crosses his arms on his chest, and closes his eyes to give up his life.

The camera is on Hoffman's face, and he is weeping. Then the camera picks up other moisture on his face, and it is apparent that it has begun to rain. The camera moves to Grandfather, and the raindrops fall on him. His eyelids twitch, the muscles in his cheeks begin to jump. He sits up and says "I didn't die, did I?"

"No, Grandfather."

"Well, . . . sometimes the magic works, and sometimes it doesn't."

He walks down the mountain again with Hoffman, saying something bawdy about his wife, right back into life again.

Sometimes the magic works and sometimes it doesn't. This is *very* important. For final exams and keynote addresses, for projects and parties and bread made from scratch. For attempts to apologize and Christmas gifts and seeds planted in the early spring.

Sometimes the magic works and sometimes it doesn't.

There is no shame in that. It is simply what life teaches us. We hurt ourselves sometimes when the magic doesn't work: the speech we give bombs, the bread falls, our efforts to reconcile only make things worse. That's when this secret can help a great deal. It is an immutable truth about life: the magic only *sometimes* works.

3

Our Gifts Don't Belong to Us

A particular facet of mixedness that has been growing in meaning for me is the paradox that our gifts do not belong to us. That certainly sounds like a cliché, but it is much more difficult to live out than to say. It hit me with great force four years ago when I was doing a long workshop on the road, and I found a message on my door that there was an emergency at home. The kids were grown, Kadee and Randy out on their own, Boo in college. I tried again and again to reach the number of anyone who might know what happened. There was no answer anywhere. Three hours went by without an answer. I was terrified that one of the children was dead. Images of them on a highway, in an emergency room, or worse, kept going through my mind.

I kept seeing their faces: Kadee, black-haired, black-eyed, laughing, enigmatic young bride. Randy, up for any adventure, blond and blue-eyed, living on an incredible sense of abiding luck. Boo, tawny-haired, brown-eyed, lean, a little shy; under the muscled body, a poet's heart.

I would picture them, and I would say inside: "God of Abraham and Isaac, start looking around for a ram. You are not going to sacrifice one of them. They are mine!"

Then I would realize they are *not* mine. They are only given to me. For a long time or a short time, they are gifts. But they do not belong to me. And I would fight to let them go.

After three hours I had a call from a neighbor. When I heard her voice I really panicked, because I knew that she must be calling because she had heard the news about one of the children.

"I have bad news for you, Pat."

"What is it, Pauline?"

"Are you sitting down?"

"What is it?"

"Your house flooded."

"That's it?"

"It's really bad. The washing machine hose must have burst days ago and water has been pouring through. It is four feet up in the walls."

"That's all? You mean that's *it*? The house?"

"Pat, you don't understand, it is really awful."

"Pauline, that's the best news I've ever had in my life."

This marvelous woman in her seventies, who loves and cares for me, knew I had totally flipped out. She was still shaking from the horror of discovering the ruin. I couldn't help it. I was in a real state of euphoria the relief was so strong. It was a powerful lightness that nothing could touch.

Gradually, the next day, I began to think about what might have been destroyed. I couldn't get home until the next week. Professional flood people were working on the mess, a team sent by my insurance company. There was nothing I could do. In fact, it was probably better that nobody was there.

But I started to imagine. I thought first about the children's pictures. They were—every one of them—in the *bottom* drawer of a desk. The notes for all my talks and workshops were in the *lower* file drawer: my whole livelihood. The little rocker from the 1700s, my one fine piece of furniture, the chair in which children of generations had been rocked—was that ruined? It was very *short.*

Then the voice began again: these things are only gifts. They do not belong to you.

As it turned out, when I got home, very little that mattered was beyond repair. The carpets were ruined; so were the curtains, wallpaper, and minor things. The walls had acted like blotters (they don't call it dry wall for nothing) and pulled the water up into them. Much of it had soaked into the carpet and drapes, lots had poured out under the front door. (The yard had never been so green!)

The strangest part is that fixing up my house was the lowest possible priority. I had had kids in college for six years, and one still had lots of time to go. Out of the flood came new paint, wallpaper, carpet, drapes, all paid for by the insurance company. The redecorating was done with the help of my friend, Dona, who is a designer with marvelous ideas and an utterly generous willingness to pass on her professional discount. The house really was lovely, with delicate colors and "grown up" designs. The era of choosing everything on the basis of whether it showed dirt was over. It was a kind of rainbow sign to me.

That story is a metaphor for me for all our gifts. They do not belong to us. Not our children, nor our parents; not our homes, nor health, nor youth; not our memory nor independence nor anyone we love. Our power does not belong to us, nor any way we have been given to use that power. It is all gift.

This has been hard for me. Sometimes I have felt possessive of my ideas or images, my designs for workshops, my style of doing things. That was especially true when I was starting out professionally. Perhaps there is a sense in which you have to hold tighter to your gifts at first because you are struggling hard to form identity.

One key funny time comes back to me. I had just given the first big keynote address of my life. It was to the North American Conference of Separated and Divorced Catholics annual meeting. I had been the first divorced person asked to keynote this annual conference. I was very honored, but also scared to death. I worked for ten months on that talk.

I wanted to end on a symbolic level, something that could really speak of the beauty and the truth of married love even though it died or failed or had been broken. I decided to use something from *Camelot* because I thought everyone would be familiar with it. Only after I chose it did I realize that it is also the story of a divorce. Of the death of a dream.

At the end Arthur is not bitter, does not wish he had never met Guinevere or Lancelot, does not regret that he ever thought of the Round Table. He is convinced that that dream, though it died, was worth dreaming; that love, though it failed, still goes on.

The very last scene shows him calling over the little sword boy, the groom for the horses, the page. He charges him to remember, from this moment on, the brief, shining splendor that Camelot once was. He commissions him to go forth and tell the story of it to every person who has not yet heard. As he sends him across the camp, into the meadow, toward the forest to tell the world, Arthur calls after him: "Run boy, run . . . run . . . run . . ."

It is a universal message for every dream that dies, for every hope that fails, for every love that somehow gets turned inside out. It is good for all kinds of gifts that we have to give back.

I tell the story because after the tape of the talk was published, a wonderful priest friend heard it. He and I were giving a workshop together for priests when he said he had decided he would use my Camelot story for his final homily.

"You what?" I replied (my tone implying that if he used my story he was more or less dead where he stood).

He roared laughing. "Pat, 100 million people have seen *Camelot*. You did not make that up! The Arthurian legend is 1500 years old! You don't own it . . . ."

We don't own our gifts. They have been given to us.

There seem to be seasons for letting go. Early parenthood is one. It is a time of utter joy and wonder that you have given birth to life, but there is a death to self that comes with a small baby that nothing else compares to. None of your time belongs to you at all. This is hardest in the hours in the night. "All the world's asleep, and I'm awake!" you think, as you get up for a feeding once again.

Another letting go is growing old. Our lives have seasons of acquiring and detaching, I read once. Detaching sounds like such a neutral word: like the tearing of the edges of a print-out, or the bottom of the power bill. There is nothing to suggest the anguish in that word. I think of one dear friend who once had lovely legs. They were her best feature, she would say. As she aged and went through mid-life childbirth the varicose veins grew dark and spreading. Then her knees began to "droop" (that's what she called it). She stopped wearing shorts, and wore her dresses long. "I hate it not to have my legs!" she'd say. Another friend had to have his teeth pulled. "An outrage!" was his comment. "Detaching" doesn't cover it.

Giving up our presence, our impact, the kind of attention we were used to getting can be cruel. My father was a man of major power in his day. As he reached his seventies, his body barely faltered, but his brain grew tangled neurons, and his mental sharpness faded.

One power he retains is buying things. He'll go to the grocery almost every day, loving the exchange with whomever is at the check-out counter.

One time when I was visiting, I went with him. He gave the money to the woman with a kind of pride, and she gave *me* the change. It hurts me even now to think of that. As if he weren't there. Going out the door he said to me "Sometimes you are invisible when you are old." Detaching.

Mother says she feels as if a lot of her has already gone over to the other side: the sharpness of her hearing and her sight, the texture of her hair, so many of her friends. "Perhaps when more of me is there than here, then I'll slide over too."

Our gifts do not belong to us. All we have and are flows out from God. The heart of faith is trusting that the central gift, our life in love, will never end.

4

Spirituality Is Not *Removed From Life*

A crucial question of life is how to understand spirituality. One of the great secrets I discovered was that spirituality is not what I once thought it was. When I would hear the term as a young person it conjured up images of a church: the flickering ruby glow of a sanctuary lamp, the long, dark shadow of a crucifix, the soft rattle of a rosary against an oak pew. I was a member of the Sodality of Our Lady in the '50s and early '60s, and spirituality involved "duties" and "practices" to be done every day: mass and meditation and spiritual reading and rosaries and visits to the blessed sacrament.

I remember feeling guilty or frustrated if the rhythms of other things got in the way of what I was supposed to do. Spirituality was something *imposed* on life. It was a piety that was somehow suspect of whatever interfered. It reflected the old duality of the holy and the worldly, the sacred and the profane.

I married right after these sodality days and soon had three preschool children, utterly disrupting this view. The idea of scheduling anything each day was almost comical.

It was very hard to get away from the view that spirituality required separate holy practices. Since that kind of structure and ritual were impossible for me, I became afraid that I was getting further and further away from God. The process of letting go of my old concept was a slow one. Only gradually did I begin to trust that instead of ordering and organizing moments of my life, life would offer those moments to me. Whenever there was a pause, a break, a little space for reflection, there could be a meeting with God—an acknowledgment of the meeting that was going on all the time.

Sometimes these moments of recollection came when I was feeding a baby in the middle of the night. Sometimes they came while folding clothes or scrubbing floors. Sometimes they came in the rare and precious privacy of the bathtub.

Probably the best of these moments was when I was stirring pudding. Everyone liked pudding. They respected the process because the result was a treat. They would hardly ever pull hair or write on walls or stick something in a socket when I was making pudding.

Pudding takes a long time. You can't leave it. I guess I've tried to sneak in just about every little task between stirrings: put in a load of clothes, take out the garbage, wash up the oatmeal pan. The minute I did, it *always* lumped. Even if it had given no sign for ten minutes of being in anything but a coma, as soon as I tried some tiny chore, it erupted into full boil—all lumps—and ran down into the burners, hardening and singeing. So standing there stirring pudding was a respite, a space to let my thoughts collect. Into those reveries would come a sense of the presence of God.

I also began to discover that I didn't have to find God. God found me. That sounds easy when you put it into words. It wasn't. The gradual daring to trust that truth came through long periods of being disheartened. But it came.

I remember one day in spring. Central Florida was already very hot. We were living in a part of Tampa that had intermittent sidewalks. I had both of the children in a stroller. The pavement had given out and I was trying to push the wheels through the sandy soil. The effort was tremendous and I was perspiring and frustrated. They were cranky and trying to pinch each other. The gnats were in our eyes.

I managed somehow to get us around a corner and there, right in front of us, was a cherry tree in full bloom. It was not a tall tree, so the branches were right above my head. The children stopped struggling and just looked. It was so unexpected and lovely, the air alive with fragrant, rose-colored lace, that tears came to my eyes. I prayed a deep thanksgiving, and it was as if God answered: "I bred that strain of cherry five thousand years ago in China for you . . . for this afternoon."

That was a kind of turning point. I knew, at least for my life, that spirituality was not something I did. It wasn't separate. It was a relating to God, responding and initiating, in the experiences of every day. It was happening all the time. I didn't know anyone else saw it that way. I wasn't even sure it was right, but it was all I had, and it brought me peace and joy.

Then one day I read a theological explanation of it. Someone had sent me Gabriel Moran's *Theology of Revelation*. I had so little time to read that I had barely been able to begin on it. I took it to the beauty parlor where I went every few months before some big event, knowing I would have some quiet there. It was under the big hair dryer that I read Moran's explanation of what I had come to in myself:

> Revelation in its most basic sense is neither a word coming down from heaven to which man assents nor an historical event manifesting a truth. It is an intersubjective communion in which man's answer is part of the revelation.[1]

I was stunned. I sat there excited and moved, confirmed on a very deep level. I didn't know until then how lonely I had felt in my struggle. My hard won private concept of spirituality as relating to God in the life of every day was what Moran was calling revelation: intersubjective communion in which my answer was a crucial part.

"This is terrific!" I said. "This is fantastic! This is it!"

When you are talking under a hair dryer, you have no idea how loud your voice is. I thought I was just speaking under my breath. I looked up and operators and customers were looking at me, a couple coming over.

"What is it? Show us."

I held up the book. I still laugh thinking of their faces.

"*Theology of Revelation*?"

They, who had been hoping for something about Jackie Kennedy or Princess Grace of Monaco, began backing up, looking at each other, rolling their eyes. They knew I had really gone off the deep end. Flipped out, poor thing.

I pored over every page of Moran's book in the next weeks. I copied out passages and reread them in doctors' offices. If I had been writing this chapter then, I would have quoted more of it. I needed that confirmation. I will always be grateful for it. It gave me confidence in what was a new territory in my life. It was a beginning for trusting my own experience of God in my life.

What I learned in those days and then had affirmed by Moran twenty years ago is even closer to me now. Spirituality is not something imposed on the present moment. It is a receptivity to God revealing God's self *in* the present moment. Instead of a controlling of the rhythms of life, it is an embracing of them. It is a "yes" to all the paradoxes and polarities, all the many dyings and risings that those moments ask of us. I have learned that death to self is far less the self-imposed penances and practices than it is a letting go in what is given and what is asked in every single day. The pattern of our lives asks of us so much more than we could ever imagine. It also gives us more than we could ever dream. Emptying us until we feel that we have lost all there is to lose. Then filling us a hundredfold, pressed down, shaken together, running over.

It has happened to me in so many scenes and styles.

Humiliating limitations and surprising strengths. Rave reviews and total bombs. Seasons of angst and times of peace. Great loneliness and incredible friendship.

I am struck by the fact that it was in the days of early motherhood that I grasped this truth in my struggle. It was somehow a gift from the children in those times of no privacy, no rest, no quiet. I could not possibly pray in the ways I had been taught in sodality. I had to let go of the concept of spirituality as set apart from life.

Now I am challenged with the living out of the truth I discovered then in a very different time in my life. It is almost the direct polarity of that early era. The children are grown. In contrast to those days long ago, when I am home now there is usually total privacy, complete quiet.

On Mother's Day, the house seemed very empty. Trying to get myself to "be sensible," I cleaned my room. I even washed the windows. I sorted through my closet and took books down from shelves to dust. Finally I cleaned my jewelry drawer. I hadn't done that in a long time. I found necklaces strung on leather thongs that had been made for me in scouting. There were dime-store Christmas earrings and colored rhinestone pins. In the very back I discovered a pair of glasses prescribed for Randy in the first grade which he absolutely refused to wear. "No sir. Not me. Never." Somehow he learned to read without them.

Finally I came across a china box with a broken lid where through the years I had put things I didn't know what else to do with. Keys for cars that had been traded in. Tags for luggage long discarded. Barrettes and bands for pony tails. And in the bottom: teeth. Tiny and very white. This is where the tooth fairy put her treasures. I had been quite unable to throw them out. I held them in my hand and tears came down my face. Where I had once met God in letting the children into my life, I stood with God in the letting go.

Life is the meeting place. Spirituality is meeting God in all that life is.

5

Sacrament Is God Revealed in Life

What I had learned in my own struggles to redefine spirituality is part of a very important truth about life—that God is revealed in every day. This strikes a very deep chord among the men and women who come to our renewal program. It isn't that they do not know this truth. Their lives have taught it to them. But to hear it confirmed and reconfirmed by speakers and by readings is very freeing. They leave with more strength and joy in the concept of sacrament.

The Catholic tradition mainly thought of sacraments in terms of the seven sacraments, the official sacred ritual acts that are seen as participation in the act of salvation itself. For most of us the bridge from sacraments to ordinary life was largely unarticulated. It would be rare that we would think out clearly, like the theologian Michael Downey, that "Sacrament is the point of connection between the invisible and the visible, the intangible and the tangible. . . . It is the point of encounter with God and human persons in community."[1]

For most of us it would have been mainly on our own, as it was for me, that we began to know that God reveals God's self in all moments and all things of our every day.

All things. I think of things like dandelions and brandy. This was a year without a spring in Indiana. Winter hung around until the edge of May, bitter and damp, with a wind that bit right through your clothes if you picked out anything that looked forward to warmth with hope. Golf and tennis had to be cancelled by all but the hardiest or most obsessed.

Then, suddenly, the cold was gone. It happened between a Monday and a Wednesday, just like that. "Ah ha," we said, "so spring has finally sprung." Well, if it did, it sprang too far. High 80s, with maximum humidity, is where it went.

"Puts you more in mind of August than of May," said the old man who runs the gas station I always go to.

I don't care what price their gas is. I hardly notice. My friends revel in the absurdity that I choose gas by personality and not by price. I really like this man. Gnarled, gruff, and strong, he must be seventy. He would have been a blacksmith if it weren't for Henry Ford. He comforts me, hunching over my windshield in his red plaid jacket. I hate pumping my own gas. Not only do I let it run over on my good shoes if I try to get it full enough to figure out how much mileage I am getting since my tune-up, I also don't have any human interchange. "Twelve forty-one on pump number three," from a woman behind a giant counter is not my idea of interchange. I love to hear "Your oil's O.K., but keep an eye out next time to be sure." I like opinions on my tires. I love to hear the weather analyzed by someone who has lived here all his life and really knows.

"Puts you more in mind of August than of May."

I liked that. It confirmed what I'd been feeling, but wouldn't have dared assert. I've only lived here three years, what do I know about their May?

What I had observed was dandelions. Maybe hot and humid after snow is dandelion paradise. On every roadside, every gully, every stretch untended in a park, dandelions crowded dandelions in ghetto density. Stalks and fluffy heads were crammed together, tens of thousands in one ditch. It used to be my job to cut them out of our front lawn when I was ten and forever after I've noticed them.

Coming out of my apartment, I saw clouds of dandelion fuzz against the wall, tumbleweeds of white. They must have mowed along the roadways. There were drifts of them: a baby boom of dandelions to come.

I felt a strong excitement. Maybe life was making a comeback. Desert Storm was barely over, the Persian Gulf polluted, the Arabian skies all blackened from the oil fires. Bangladesh was devastated by a cyclone, the crops destroyed. Kurds were freezing in the mountains. The world was filled with death, and here were mounds of dandelions insisting there was life. Nothing holds on to life as fiercely as a dandelion. A sacrament.

One winter I had another kind of revelation moment around brandy. I was looking through a catalog and saw an ad for a brandy warmer, a metal frame with a lighter in the base in which to set a snifter. I looked at it a long time. I was feeling exhausted. It had been a fall with crazy schedules and lots of unexpected crises. It wasn't really the brandy that drew me (it tends to make me choke), but the leisure, the idea of time, time to warm the brandy with a friend.

I tried it. I ordered two, and gathered special people. We poured the liquid in the glass and lit the fire, put the snifter in the cradle. I've never understood what happened next. A great fire sprung—perhaps the fuel was wrong. Flames blazed up and turned the ceiling black. The kids all home from college yelled: "Get marshmallows, quick!"

Somehow we got the fire out, and laughed and laughed. I felt all the tightness in me just shake loose. We wanted to be elegant, and ended up hilarious instead. We drank some brandy plain, ate marshmallows from a box, and heard (we thought) the chuckling of God.

Theologian Michael Himes is one of the great favorites in our sabbatical program. He speaks of grace as everywhere. He explains that sacraments embody grace by making grace present to us, by helping us to notice it in a particular time and place, pointing to the fact that it is at all times, everywhere.

Creation, he says, is everything that exists that is not God. All that exists, God loved into being. If God did not love it, it would not exist. "As simple as that," Himes would say with his accent that is Britain and Brooklyn all at once. "Everything has existence because God loves it: the farthest supernova, the last dinosaur, your favorite rhododendron, your pet cat."

A sacrament is something that calls our attention to God's present love. "It makes something more real by pointing to it," Himes says. Anything can be sacramental if attended to. He quotes Gerard Manley Hopkins' poem "Hurrahing in Harvest." Hopkins was dreading the winter and not even noticing the glory of fall. Suddenly he began to see the autumn, to focus on the beauty of the harvest that he had not seen before.

> These things,
> these things were here and but the beholder
> Wanting.

Sacraments call out our beholding. All aestheticism is a training in beholding. To really *see* reality, see things as they are, is to see the love of God embodied, the grace of God displayed before us.

Alice Walker understands this. In *The Color Purple* she has Shug say to Celie:

> "I think it pisses God off if you walk by the color purple in a field somewhere and don't notice it."
>
> "What do it do when it pissed off?" Celie asks.
>
> "Oh, it make something else. People think pleasing God is all God care about. But any fool living in the world can see it always trying to please us back."
>
> "Yeah?" I say.
>
> "Yeah," she say. "It always making little surprises and springing them on us when us least expect."[2]

A beloved friend of mine has a phrase for this. She is in her nineties, a Religious of the Sacred Heart. She taught me when I was in high school, and is the closest person to a mentor I've ever had. I was long grown up before I understood some of the things she said to me, but in times of struggle to find meaning, I would remember. She is from New Orleans, and has its splendid accent. Her name is Mother Mouton.

Last year I gave a workshop near the retirement home her order has in California. As soon as morning class was over, I dropped in to see if I could find her. She had just been going in to lunch, and invited me to join her in a private room. We were enthralled to see each other, and spent the whole hour from one topic to another catching up. Her spine is bent with osteoporosis. When she stands she's almost double, but when she sits and looks at you her brown eyes are absolutely clear.

"You know what this is, my darling Pat?" (She always talks that way, the French custom of address forming her style. She spoke French until she went to school.) "It is *la delicatesse du Bon Dieu.* For you to come today is grace itself, a day there was only green Jell-O for dessert for lunch." She laughed and laughed. She wouldn't dream of complaining about food. But she notices.

We need to learn to notice. We need to contemplate, to open ourselves to what Hopkins calls "beholding." We need to learn to see the revelation of splendid tenderness: *la delicatesse du Bon Dieu.*

The Catholic tradition has said that grace builds on nature: nature itself is good. Himes says that for nature to exist at all it must be graced; God must love it for it to exist, so grace really builds on grace.

Eugene Lauer, theologian and director of our program, teaches our course on sacraments. He underscores the fact that in our Catholic understanding of scripture, everything reflects God. All creation is good. Every thing, every person, has the innate potential of reflecting the divine, of being an encounter with the divine, of being the intimate touch of the divine. "Look inside creation: God is there."

To look inside creation takes a special kind of seeing. What e.e. cummings calls "the eyes of our eyes," must be open. Elizabeth Barrett Browning spoke of this when she wrote in "Aurora Leigh":

> Earth is crammed with heaven,
> And every common bush afire with God;
> But only he who sees takes off his shoes,
> And all the rest stand around picking blueberries.

That all creation reveals God is what Andrew Greeley calls "the Catholic sensibility." Our tradition incorporates the enormous religious importance of experience and imagination. It is filled with created things to help us contact God: holy water, candles, flowers, saints, rosary beads, incense, ashes, Christmas cribs, stained glass, music.

There is great power in creation, as Annie Dillard expresses in *Pilgrim at Tinker Creek:*

> The extravagant gesture is the very stuff of creation. After the one extravagant gesture of creation in the first place, the universe has continued to deal exclusively in extravagances, flinging intricacies and colossi down aeons of emptiness, heaping profusions on profligacies with ever fresh vigor. The whole show has been on fire from the word go![3]

We cannot always sense the power in the every day. Our lives dull us with their relentless demands—their repetition wearing us down. James Carroll speaks of this in *The Winter Name of God*. He describes how there are seasons in our lives when we grow cold and stark and bleak, and a winter comes upon us. After what always seems like a long time something happens. Something stirs and quickens. There is a freshening. He declares that "freshness" *is* the winter name of God.

The freshness, the spiriting, comes through our dry bones and breathes life into them again. It happened to me yesterday. I was out walking early, before it grew too hot in this

Florida July. Without notice it began to rain. At first I struggled, trying to avoid it, running, pulling my shirt up over my head. But then I just let go and let the wetness take me. The rain was warm and mild, the wind was soft, a friendly touch of earth and sky. I put my face up to the clouds and tried to greet the touch.

Memories poured through me, scenes I had forgotten from the past. When we were young we often played in summer rain in our walled garden in Japan. We pretended we were fairy children in a dell, or covered wagon pioneers unsheltered on a plain. Later, when we moved back to Washington, there was an alley behind the tudor row house where we lived. Its paved stretch divided the houses from the yards beyond, running between lawns and flowers on either side. The alley was a hill, and storms would send a river down its curve. As soon as lightning stopped we would run out in the downpour, splash, and feel the elemental force.

My younger sister, Mary Lee, would lead us. She is a poet, photographer, and artist, passionately connected to the earth. "Let's go!" she'd shout, "before the rain stops! Come!" I had forgotten that. Next I remembered when she led that same charge once when we were grown and she had come to visit. She ran out in the yard into an utter deluge, calling, laughing, to the window. "Come out!! You don't know what you're missing!" She hugged me and the kids as we dashed out. It was glorious. We stayed out for an hour.

All of that came back just yesterday, walking in the rain: a familiar, primal, elfin feeling pouring through my soul. The freshening.

Children are direct lines into freshness. Their language is brand new, and so they say things not yet worn. "My hands get fragile when I giggle," Kadee said at five, in that weak-from-laughing state. "Valentines have ears," she observed, cutting out the shape to paste on paper lace.

Looking at me solemnly over the rim of a cup of Kool-Aid, Boo, at three, informed me, "I am drinking my coffee break." Later on that day, a day of gray and wind, he made the observation, "The lake is wrinkled."

"The moon is broke," said Randy, four years old, when the last time he had noticed it the moon was full. "And Wesley did it!" (Wesley was a boy across the street he did not like.) "Fe, fi, fo, fum, I smell the blood of an English muffin!" was Randy's chant those days.

Freshness is found in the things that children do as well as say. One incident that I remember clearly was a grace. Kadee was a climber. When she could barely walk, she was up on everything. What she could not reach alone, she'd push chairs over to and scale. She loved to jump to you from up on high, from tables or counters or desks.

One night we had invited a neighbor in for supper. He lived downstairs in the near-campus housing, a law student. He was blind. He rang the door bell, and shortly after I let him in, the timer rang on the stove and I dashed into the kitchen to take the biscuits out. In my absence Kadee climbed up on the sideboard, and with a gleeful laugh, jumped off to him. He was stunned. Of course, he couldn't see her, so had no idea she was about to leap. His arms went up and caught her and she yelled: "Hooray!" I had glimpsed it from the kitchen doorway, too far away to intervene. His face was gray with fright. What if he'd dropped her? Then suddenly he smiled. He *hadn't* dropped her! She had trusted him. She didn't know his handicap, and treated him as if he could, of course, be played with. I can still see the kind of pride that transfixed his features. The touch of God.

Jesus is the ultimate sacrament. Jesus is God in the human condition. His incarnation intensifies the reality of God with us. Kathleen Chesto writes:

> I suspect Jesus was never more human than on the night before he died. Gathering his dearest friends around him, he wondered the same things each of us wonder in the face of death: "Will anyone remember me when I am gone, will anything I have done make any difference at all?"

> Then he took bread, blessed it and broke it, and taught us, when there are no more deeds to be done, no more miracles to be worked, no more parables to be spoken, the greatest gift remains to be given: Real Presence. It is the gift each of us can give. . . .[4]

I am thinking of my father. His brain is miswired with advancing Alzheimer's and he cannot really follow conversation much. It doesn't matter. He looks at us, he nods, sometimes he puts in a word or two. If he can't think of a word, he makes one up quite easily. He is very present. I learned years ago teaching communication skills that experts have proved that communication is 92 percent body language and voice tone, and only 8 percent content. Dad is missing most of the 8 percent, but much of the 92 percent is still quite there. We feel his presence strongly, the love and gift of it.

Some people's presence is in their smile. In Reynolds Price's book, *Kate Vaiden,* there is a line I love: "His smile'd grow roses on rusty barbed-wire."

My grandfather used to have it in his voice. It was a rough, kind voice, a little hoarse, with tones and timbre that would sort of reach around you. A voice to feel belonging in. A voice that could correct you, but still convey that you were very welcome as you were. The phrase he said the most, a phrase of utter presence in its simplicity, was his response to something you had said. I'd tell him things, complain, describe, exclaim, or share a secret. He would look at me, and say, "Well, think of that!" As if what you had told him was amazing and important. That husky pitch was presence sounded out.

Wherever loving presence is, there we find God. That is the ancient faith statement, sung as a hymn by the earliest Christians, written in the first letter of John: *Ubi caritas, deus ibi est.* Wherever love is, there is God (cf. 1 Jn 4:16).

It is a particular kind of love, merciful, forgiving, a love that eats and drinks together, a place where there can be exchange of nourishment.

Food is so important. We lose sight of this in a culture where trying to diet is more of a challenge than trying not to go hungry. Food and sharing food are crucial sacraments. Jesus, appearing after his death, came to his disciples on the beach. His question was "Have you anything to eat?"

A thousand images are conjured up in me with that. I heard that question almost hourly when the children were at home. I always smile at liturgy when the priest says right before communion: "Happy are we who are called to this supper." The relief and joy of being called to supper, the squeals of "it's ready now!", the choruses from *Oliver* of "Food, glorious food!" echo through my mind. I've never thought that line was said by celebrants with the emphasis of someone who had done much calling to the table.

Sharing food can be such a sacrament. Soup kitchen lines and picnics, popcorn in a movie and cookies after school, waffles after church on Sunday, and dinner with someone finally home again.

Not long ago we gathered for my parents' fiftieth wedding anniversary. I can still see the table set with Spode and silver, narcissus in a simple vase, honeyed, spiraled ham on a great platter. There were piles of presents. My younger sister had assembled a "trousseau" for mom to open, as many things as possible were yellow or gold for the occasion: a quilted bathrobe, a fake fur coat, a dress and jacket, teddies and garter belts with lace. The whole occasion was a banquet, blocking for that afternoon the reality of the illnesses that so depleted both of them that they could no longer live together.

Another moment comes to my mind from long ago. I was six months pregnant with my firstborn. At Ft. Bragg Army Hospital all the pregnant women would line up along a wall waiting to see a doctor. You had to weigh in first, your gain or loss recorded on your chart. One day there were at least twelve of us, all weighed in for the week, all waiting. "Quick, no one's looking," said a Hispanic woman, pregnant with her third. She took out of her purse a bag of Milky Ways and passed them all around. "Take two!" she said. "They cannot weigh us 'til next week." It was such communion, eating candy bars together in the gray-green of that hall.

Teilhard de Chardin writes in *The Divine Milieu* that inherent in creation is the evolving toward the divine, Christ directing the evolutionary process to God, Christ redeeming physical creation as well as human beings. After the incarnation, the presence of God in the universe is Christ, Chardin says. We are all involved in redemption, in the gathering into a loving union, with Christ. Christ is very much alive in each and all of us created things.

I had a powerful experience of the vitality of Christ in the midst of creation last Christmas Eve. I had gotten home to Florida just the day before. I wanted to go to midnight mass, and just by luck discovered that it had been moved to nine p.m. (I groaned. My friends up north all tease me that I live in such a small town the restaurants close by seven. How they would hoot at midnight mass being held at nine!)

The altar was tied with red velvet ribbon like a package; beside it a blue spruce was covered with bows and lights. The crib was in front of three tall pine trees and a potted palm. I wondered what it had been like in Bethlehem. Palm trees were likely, I reflected. The pastor greeted us, then gave a stern lecture against leaving early. I shifted in my seat. The lector began, the microphone acting up, the static in a rhythm.

A little choir of adults and children started singing "A baby came like a violet in the snow," and a procession moved through the church to form a pageant. Shepherds, angels, wise men. Last came the three, Joseph, Mary, Jesus. As they passed me, I was stunned to realize there was a real baby, newly born from the look of it.

The young woman playing Mary held it all through mass. She sat there with great poise, her face reflective, lovely framed in blue. The baby never cried. I was enormously touched by the two of them, and by Joseph, another high school student, patient, collected, standing still. As I was leaving, the marvelous woman who is our pastoral associate,

Sister Mary Ann, told me about the baby. The baptism had been the previous Sunday. The baby was a girl. She was Hispanic. She had Down's syndrome. Tears came to my eyes. The Christmas truth: God exists in all of us. We are all Christ in creation. Everyone.

6

Mercy Is God's Clearest Sign

All creation shines forth God, but perhaps the clearest sign of God is mercy.

How do we know if something is from God? The test, the trial it must pass is this: "Does it feed life?" The ancient way people recognized Jesus was that he fed them: in the breaking of the bread, in the words that made their hearts burn within them on the road. Our central Christian ritual is a meal.

What seems to feed life most of all is mercy. Meister Eckhart says "You may call God love, you may call God goodness. But the best name for God is compassion."[1]

I talked with Marilyn Schaub, the delightful archeologist and scripture scholar who teaches the prophets course in our program, about the Hebrew word for mercy. She told me it is *rachamim*, meaning mercy, tenderness, or compassion. "It is derived," she said with her most engaging smile, knowing she was giving me a significant surprise, "from the word *rechem*, which means womb."

Mercy, seen through that Hebrew image, comes from the very depths of God, from the place that life itself is conceived and carried and born. When we are treated with mercy, it is as if we are received in our pain or our guilt into the womb of God. We are nourished and rocked in the fluids of God's being, protected and held while we grow strong, and then brought forth to life again. This image has the richest human sense of what it means to feed life.

Thomas Merton also sees mercy as the feminine in God, as Sophia, the name of God from the book of Wisdom. In his poem "Hagia Sophia," Merton says: "Sophia is the mercy of God in us, the tenderness with which the infinitely mysterious power of pardon turns the darkness of our sins into the power of grace."[2]

Something happens in us in the presence of mercy: both in the giving and receiving. It is as Ezekiel's Yahweh says: "I shall remove the heart of stone from your bodies and give you a heart of flesh instead" (Ez 36:26). In whatever kind of pain or sin, whatever difficulty has isolated us or turned our hearts to stone, we are offered a transformation into loving life. In the metaphor of *rachamim,* we are warmed in the womb of God.

Schaub explains that an important part of the Hebrew understanding was that mercy was not thought of as God's response to an offense, or as an action won from God in our need through sacrifice or appeasement. Mercy flowed from God's initiative, God always taking the first step to bestow tenderness on the other.

We can experience the power of mercy even in very small things. I felt it once on a very hassled day when everything that could go wrong lined up to be the next to do so. I felt tight and tense, my face severe. Five teen-aged boys were at the house. I was bracing against their noise, against the mess I knew they'd make. One of them, a friend of Randy's, stuck his head in my room's doorway to say hello. Maybe the stress was in my voice when I replied. But instead of calling, "Lighten up! Hey, Mrs. L. don't be a drag," he walked in and looked at me. "How are you doing?" he said, and watched me closely. "How are things for you these days? Are you O.K.?" He stood there, still, prepared to listen.

It was a little thing, but I still remember how it felt.

Instead of making fun of me for my uptightness, he asked me how I was. I said something simple, like "I'm working hard," and smiled at him, releasing him to join the other boys. But I felt the mercy.

Mercy can be food brought when you are weak or tired. I have a Cuban friend, a fascinating woman, who brings me café con leche when I'm sad sometimes. I have another friend who brought me homemade soup in a huge thermos when I was in the hospital. I'm convinced it made me well.

Another source of mercy has been someone showing me practical things that I couldn't discover on my own. A Q-tip dipped in Clorox will take black marker ink out of a white skirt. White vinegar will get minerals from the water out of pots and pans. Suntan lotion will take tar off feet at the seashore. Having these small saving things passed on to me has felt life-giving.

Humor is such a source of mercy. So much pain and worry, so many fears and tense frustrations move into perspective when we really laugh. It can be over little things, silly situations, tiny jokes. I howled last week when a friend's third grade son asked me, "What is 'ha, ha, plop'?"

"I don't know, what is it?"

"Someone laughing their head off," he replied. "What is 10 . . . 9 . . . 8 . . . 7 . . . 6 . . . 5 . . . 4 . . . 3 . . . 2 . . . 1 . . . 0 . . . ?" his older sister asked.

"A countdown?"

"No. It's Bo Derrick growing old."

Simple things. (Stupid things, some have suggested!) But I have found them lightening.

It's an exquisite mercy to laugh at ourselves. A woman in a nursing home told me this story. I wish I could convey the delight she took in it. She is a person who struggles with her short-term memory. She deals with it by trying to be humorous. ("My memory is so bad, I forgot the Alamo," is one of her lines.)

Her joke was this:

A man went to visit his aunt in a nursing home. She said

to him, "Where is Uncle Benny?"

"Well, Aunt Sue, Uncle Benny died."

"What about Ralph? Where's Ralph?"

"I'm afraid Ralph's gone, too."

"What about my sister Janie? I never see her around here."

"Oh, Aunt Sue, I'm sorry. Jane died too."

"What the hell happened? Was there a massacre?"

This tiny woman in her gingham bathrobe laughed and laughed. We laughed together. It felt like mercy.

In the third book of Tolkien's *The Lord of the Rings* trilogy, Frodo and Sam have completed the destruction of the Ring of Power, thus breaking the force of evil and bringing an end to the despair that filled Middle Earth. They have been through endless trials with terrifying encounters. Utterly exhausting every resource of body and spirit, they fall unconscious just outside the mountain of the fires of Mordor. Eagles carry them to safety. Sam wakes up to find Gandalf the Wizard speaking to him. He had last seen Gandalf fall into oblivion from a bridge in the heart of a mountain.

> "Gandalf! I thought you were dead! But then I thought I was dead myself. Is everything sad going to come untrue? What's happened to the world?"
>
> "A great shadow has departed," said Gandalf, and then he laughed, and the sound was like music, or like water in a parched land; and as he listened the thought came to Sam that he had not heard laughter, the pure sound of merriment, for days upon days without count. It fell on his ears like the echo of all the joys he had ever known.[3]

Sometimes the mercy is a gift of pride. Some years ago the Special Olympics were held at the University of Notre Dame. A Holy Cross sister in her eighties told me this story. She said that hundreds of boys and girls with varying handicaps came from all over the country. I asked her if she went to the competitions. "Oh yes," she said, "I took part in it. I was a hugger. My job was to cheer and hug people when they came across the line. I was assigned a boy or a girl in each event to cheer for and to hug."

She told me about one race in which a boy was way out ahead. He would plainly come across the finish line minutes before any of the others. He turned around to see what the others were doing. He noticed a small boy whom he had come to know in the qualifying trials. The boy had tripped and fallen. The runner in front turned around and went back and picked the boy up and carried him across the line. They came in last. The cheers from the crowd filled the summer sky.

"He was my boy, the one for me to hug," my friend said, at our table in the cafeteria, her short modernized veil framing her lovely face. "Can you imagine how I felt? I was awestruck by his mercy."

People see each other fallen, and they give a hand. I was in a summer program once with a woman from Argentina. She was striking—dark and graceful. She wore a red shawl sometimes, and when she walked in a room, her life force turned us all in her direction. In that same group there was a man who had been a priest for more than forty years. He was stern, spoke gruffly, said things just to shock us. He was big and tall and very strong. His eyebrows were quite black, and when he scowled, they met above his eyes. Juanita (I will call her) spotted him the very day they came. She knew early this was a man who had been hurt. He did not have to tell her about a vicious father and an adolescence in a brutal seminary. She could tell the story from his eyes.

She had a lovely pretense that she used. Trying to improve her English, she would watch a soap opera when lunch was over. She asked him if he'd join her, and explain the words she didn't know. They watched the program every day together, just the two of them. The stories were of fights and love and uproar. Rampant feelings portrayed before this guarded man. They would talk about the characters together, those people in the stories—*novellas* she called them. Day after day, week after week, they watched and talked. Her

English flourished. His eyes began to shine.

When the summer session ended, he announced to all of us: "I want to thank Juanita in front of all the group. She befriended me. This seems like a ridiculous thing for a man my age to say, but it is important to me to say it. Because of her, I know for the first time, really, in my life that I'm worthwhile." His gruff voice almost broke. She raised her head, and grinned, the red shawl draped around her with a flair. "You really are," she said. "My English is now esplendid!" We all applauded and the dinner line began. In those warm months it was mercy she had offered him.

Sometimes the mercy is very subtle. It can happen from a stranger on an airplane. I remember one week of being on the road when I was very tired. It had been a month of significant plane crashes, and now it was a week of storms. Sometimes thunderstorms can be more disruptive to airport schedules than a snowstorm. Twenty flights cannot take off, and the whole system in the country is fouled up for hours. I was on a flight from Dayton to La Guardia, a Friday night, and was feeling almost smug that we loaded in Dayton right on time. Other flights were delayed as they waited for people off flights that hadn't come in yet. But our flight was there; we boarded, buckled up, pushed back from the gate. And then we sat. Twenty minutes, thirty minutes, forty minutes, on the runway. There were babies at all four compass points, all yelling. Not infants, but two-year-olds. One would shriek and set the others off.

Finally we were in the air. A snack was served. The family behind me had a vegetarian meal that they had ordered. The woman next to me, who had complained in nasal fury whenever one of the children nudged her seat, demanded from the steward a special snack as well.

"You have to order it ahead," he said.

"But I want it now," she countermanded. "I am a real vegetarian, I deserve it."

"It's not a question of deserve," he said with all the patience he could manage. "We do not have it on the plane."

As we got in the airspace near New York we banked and turned in arcs. The pilot explained we'd have to circle quite a while.

"I gotta get outta here," a yuppy-looking redhead said between his teeth. All four toddlers screamed at once.

On almost the last lap of the circling, the child behind me stood and threw up her vegetarian snack on her mother and her father and the carpet.

We landed, and there was another aircraft at our gate. We were delayed ten minutes more. When we finally began to pull up to the gate, we were informed that the jetway was not working.

"We'll have to deplane from the rear of the craft," said the stewardess. The yuppy got up, grabbed his carry-on, and bolted to the back.

"Sit down, sir, you must sit down. We are still on an active runway." He ignored the stewardess totally.

It was an awful time. Sitting one row ahead of me on the aisle was a woman I had noticed back in Dayton. She seemed to be mid-thirties, dressed in linen, cream and gray. She wore white hose over tanned legs, soft cream shoes. Her hair was blonde, cut beautifully to suit her face. Her jewelry had a simple elegance, her make-up just exactly right. She had been talking with some business people, sounding very quick and clever, while I watched her in that airport. Her briefcase matched her bag. I had felt a stab of envy, and pegged her for a snob.

On the flight she was next to a tired mother and a very bratty little girl. The mother had no energy to offer, so the girl turned to the woman on the aisle.

"Read this to me. Color this. What's in your bag? Who are you?"

I watched it, fascinated. The woman in linen read and colored, talked and laughed at jokes. When the child behind me threw up, she was encouraging and humorous and without judgment. She was also empathic with the yuppy man.

"He must not have kids," she said to us. "Poor guy. He'll probably never have them now! He's just not used to this. It's understandable." Her saying that helped me have a little room for him. I had been thinking he was acting like a kid himself.

When the jetway in the back still did not work, the griping in the cabin went to fever pitch. In its midst she said, with no moralizing tone at all, just frankly, "I've been on seven planes this week, I'm just so glad we're safely home."

I could feel a shift in attitude spread out among us. What did this last inconvenience matter anyway? The hostile tensing eased. It felt like she had called us into mercy. The yuppy was the first one off at last.

Often mercy is within families. Recently I heard a story about a daughter of a friend of mine. The young woman had finished college for the year and answered a phone call late one afternoon. It was her grandfather. His fiftieth reunion at Harvard was the next month and he had decided he would go.

It sounded like a simple thing but she knew it was not. He had had a breakdown in his twenties when her mother was very young. It ended with his being institutionalized, and he was only released when the big hospitals emptied into small care homes. He still heard voices, still paced furrows in the rugs, still struggled with a paranoia that kept him tense and wary. For him to take a train and then a bus and then figure out the complexity reunions always are, was a task too huge for success. Swallowing a surge of dread, she said into the phone: "What if I went with you, Grandpa?"

She did it. She picked him up and drove him all the way to Harvard, stopping every half an hour because of his incontinence. She checked them in, located his old friends, scouted out the schedule. Only late that night did she discover he had not brought his medicine that he had to take every day. She called the place he lived and got the name of the drug. Appealing to the chairman of the reunion, an M.D. of many years, she managed a prescription.

At the luncheon the next day she discovered that her way had not been paid. After buying the medicine, she was down to fifteen dollars and some change. She knew her grandfather couldn't really manage the activities without her. The chairman noticed her alarm, and told her the class would be honored to have her as their guest.

She went with her grandfather all week to all the things he wanted. He never had an accident. He hardly ever spoke aloud to voices other people could not hear. "It was hard," she told me later. "The nights were worst. He barely sleeps."

I knew this young woman when she was a child. She might have been the greatest challenge born. She took the boat out in the middle of the lake in thunderstorms. At three she climbed a palm tree, and got stuck, unable to back down because the sharp-edged bark grows up. That same year she crept downstairs after her parents went to sleep after a party. She finished what was left in every wine glass, and walked downtown at three a.m. There was nothing she could not think up, and most of what she thought of she would try. Her I.Q. was genius level, and adventure was what every day was for. As she grew up, she mellowed, learned to discipline herself. Raw power turned itself to strength.

When she was leaving Harvard with her grandpa, the chairman called her over. "Young woman may I tell you something? Most of us who came here have had children. We have grandchildren, some even great-grandchildren. Few of us have any offspring who would come with us, even for an evening. Many of them barely acknowledge we're alive. For most of us the best part of this reunion was that you were here with him and us. We're proud of you and him."

Mercy touches deeply when it comes.

Mercy acknowledges the other as having human dignity. Children sometimes do this. I saw it once with Liza long ago. She is my older sister's older daughter, out of college now, but then about two and a half. My family was in the middle of a move from east to west, and had stopped in New Orleans where my sister and her husband lived that year.

We had gone to a marvelous place in the French Quarter for beignets, those square doughnuts that make you think you would give anything to have been born a Cajun. All of a sudden at the table Liza got a very intense look on her face and said she had to go to the potty. I had already checked out the bathrooms and they were very dirty. It is very hard for someone two years old to avoid sitting on a toilet seat. I remembered that we had a portable potty in our station wagon, which was parked not too far away.

"Come with me, Liza," I said, "We'll use the potty in our car."

"As long as we can do it fast," she said.

We hurried off, with my carrying her the last block. I struggled to get the car key out and set the potty on the floor in the back. Just then a wino walked up, a hideously filthy man, his pants held up with string, his shirt torn and smeared with parts of meals and sloshed wine. He had no teeth, and made some kind of guttural sounds in our direction. I did not want him to witness our activity, but there was nothing to do about it. Liza had waited as long as she could. I tried to shield her from his gaze as I helped her out of her red tights and lace trimmed panties. He only shifted so he could stare at her, drooling now, and making obscene groans. I was terrified.

At that moment, Liza, sitting with great relief at last on the potty, looked up at him. She had the most remarkable perfectly round blue eyes with long dark lashes. Her hair was thick and blonde in bright braids. She had pink cheeks, what writers call apple cheeks. She looked at him with those eyes and a beatific smile curving those cheeks and said, "It's all right, you know, we have our own potty here."

That old man, older than his years, older than any person should ever have to get, knew what she meant. It had been years probably since he had had his own bathroom. He knew what it meant to be chased out of alleys and doorways and phone booths where he was trying to relieve himself.

Something happened as Liza looked at him, radiant with trust, totally without judgment, explaining with certain confidentiality that she knew he would understand that this was O.K. To her he was a person like she was, and persons know these things. In that exchange he came into the human race again. The sound he made was one of such tenderness and understanding that I cannot think of it even now without an ache in my throat. He was a person given mercy.

7

Forgiveness Interweaves With Mercy

Mercy is interwoven with forgiveness. Forgiveness has a key role in the teaching of Jesus. So few things were commanded: eat my body, drink my blood; wash each others' feet; forgive. Under questioning about how many times we should forgive, Jesus responded with a metaphor that meant as many times as there is need.

Why is forgiveness so important? This is something that fascinates me, and I have talked about it many times with friends or groups in workshops. When we exchange why we think it is important, powerful learnings pour out, each one gleaned from a story.[1]

If the hurt is deep, forgiveness is terribly hard. One friend said, "Forgiveness forces me to need God. I could never do it alone. I am thrown into the dependence that puts my whole life in perspective."

Another said, "*Not* forgiving poisons my world." Hardened hearts block love. Anger, resentment, and hatred take up room love cannot occupy. They give our bodies pain and illness. (Migraines, arthritis, back pain, even cancer have been related to refusing to forgive.)

Another friend, a priest who had been brutally mugged, said "Not forgiving keeps the pain alive. They hurt me once, but every time I held on to it, replaying it, I hurt myself again. I let their violence have continuing power over me."

Once we forgive something, we have a kind of *largerness*, a roomier soul. Smaller things get easier. A woman said to me once: "I forgave my husband for having an affair. I guess I can forgive my daughter for taking my green earrings without asking."

A final thing has been very important for me. When I forgive, I have to give up being "right." A friend said to me once when we were having a fight, "Do you want to be right, or do you want to work this out?"

I don't mean we shouldn't be assertive, I don't mean we shouldn't stand up for things that are important to us, I don't think we should have a lifestyle of "giving in." I'm trying to describe a stance of wounded righteousness, a victim role, where we retreat with our offendedness to a holy height. My sister once said to me: "You're right, that's true, but somehow you are not that right." The place of righteous, one-up indignation can be sterile and inflexible. It is not necessarily something to organize our personality around. It's not a very good hearth at the center of our soul. A lot of other places can be a lot more fun.

Why is it important to let someone else ask our forgiveness?

Erich Segal wrote in *Love Story* that "love means never having to say you're sorry." That, for me, is totally untrue. Love is all about having to say you're sorry. And letting people say it to you.

The first Christmas after Kadee was married she and her husband John came over early to open presents with me and the boys. The boys were still asleep, so we got a start on making breakfast. While she was helping pour popover dough into the pans, she said "Remember the Christmas you only got one present, a box of candy, and while you were doing the dishes we ate all the good pieces?"

"Yes, I remember." There had been a lot of reasons why that was a hard Christmas.

"You cried," she said. I hated it that she remembered that. "I really ate most of them," she said. "I'm sorry."

We gave each other a huge hug.

Half an hour later I was opening a box from her. It was one of those decorative boxes for Christmas goodies they sell at Hallmark stores, a deep, narrow box with a top that fitted together like a bow. Inside were chocolates, the same kind from years ago: Mrs. See's, they were called. There were only the good pieces: caramel layered with marshmallow, raspberry cordial, cashews in dark chocolate. The note said "It is time you got these back."

I was so touched I couldn't even speak. My hurt that the kids had eaten my candy had been very brief. I had let go of it completely at that time. I would never have thought of it again if she had not brought it up. But she remembered and felt badly all those years.

Allowing people to ask forgiveness helps the person who has offended let go of shame and guilt. It begins to relieve the awkwardness we feel. There is a possibility for a real exchange of love. They have a chance to say: "I love you and I hate it that I hurt you, or I let you down." We have a chance to say: "I love you, and I won't let anything keep separating us. You don't have to be perfect for me to love you."

The Christmas Kadee gave me back the chocolates was one of the most powerful exchanges we ever had. I thought of the old Latin phrase: *felix culpa,* the happy fault. The reconciling love was much stronger than ever the hurt had been hard.

Forgiveness is a cornerstone of love. I don't think I have ever felt so grateful, so freed, as when someone I wronged forgave me graciously. It was as if a terrible pervasive ugliness were lifted.

When we first came to Florida to live, over twenty years ago, the Everglades caught fire one spring. It turns out that decayed vegetation is very combustible! The fire lasted weeks and weeks and the thick smoke blocked the sky. If you were near, it burned your eyes and throat. People who came to Florida for vacation turned around and left. One day, veiled by smoke and so unseen, thunderheads gathered in the sky. Lightning came through the smog, and it began to rain. Solid rain, constant rain, a night and day and night of rain. Suddenly the air was cleared, the acrid pall was gone, a freshness spread. The fire was out.

The mercy of forgiveness is like that.

Finally, it is crucial that we forgive ourselves. If we will not, if we hate ourselves, God's love cannot get in. It is the only thing that blocks God's love. I knew an old Brother who was terrified to die. He said he knew he was going to hell. He had confessed over and over, but it did no good. After sixty-five years of selfless giving in the missions, he was still convinced that he was bad. He could not forgive himself.

I call that hatred of ourselves, that soul-corroding guilt, the Ogre. It takes us over. It waits beside our bed, with fangs and talons, ready to pounce when we awake.

One day I was working at home and the doorbell rang. When I answered it, there stood Sarah, a young woman who had been our babysitter years before. She had been marvelous with the children, responsible and funny. She would have been worth the money just for how clean she left the kitchen. She would even sort out the utensil drawer. In all the years she was our favorite.

I hadn't seen her in a long time. I had heard she had had a breakdown and had been in the hospital. She stood in the doorway looking very nervous. In her hand was a folded ten dollar bill which she held out to me.

"I want to pay this back to you, Mrs. Livingston," she said. "It's for the candy I stole when I babysat for you all."

"Oh Sarah, don't be silly. If you managed to get any candy before the kids all wiped it out, more power to you!"

"Oh no," she argued, "I did steal it. If you had wanted me to have it you would have told me. Please take the money."

"This is really important to you, isn't it?"

"It is."

"Well, Sarah, I don't think in any way you stole from me, but if you want me to take it, I will take it."She was clearly glad when I let her put it in my hand. Then she got very serious again: "I know that's why you and Mr. Livingston got a divorce."

"I beg your pardon?"

"Because of the candy. You thought he took it, and he thought you took it, and that's why you got a divorce. It was my fault."

"Oh Sarah, darling child," I said, gathering her in my arms. "Our divorce had nothing to do with you. Our troubles began before we ever knew you. We were just too different from each other. Two good people, but very, very different. It wasn't anybody's fault."

I could feel her body relax. I looked down at her face and saw relief and joy for just a minute. Then she tightened up again. "But the candy was one more thing. You had made it that far, and then the candy was one more thing."

I just looked at her with a terrible sadness. I could not make her believe it. Nothing I could do or say could show her that she was totally innocent, utterly dear, free from any possible guilt. The Ogre had her in its grip.

God tries so hard to free us. We need to hear St. Paul:

> For I am certain of this: neither death nor life, no angel, no prince, nothing that exists, nothing still to come, not any power, or height or depth, nor any created thing, can ever come between us and the love of God made visible in Christ Jesus our Lord (Rom 8:38-39, *JB*).

8

Suffering Can Lead to Life

In the reflection on sacramentality, we spoke of the goodness of reality shining forth the face of God. Images of grace come to mind. Just now I am remembering a greeting I got one spring from my friend Mary's daughter, Laura (the younger sister of Megan who once had a three-year-old thumb in a four-year-old mouth.) Laura was about five, and when I drove up and got out of my car, she ran and hugged me, then started spinning around in the grass saying: "Daffodils and tulips and violets and you, all in one day!" For me it was a greeting of enormous grace, the sudden touch of goodness in reality.

But what about the evil in reality? Yesterday was July 4th, and after sundown we gathered on the shore of the little lake our town is built around to watch the fireworks. They were the best I've ever seen: not too many, not too long, beautifully selected and set off. I felt the same deep wonder I remember as a child of four at the great explosions of flowering stars, gold and silver, green and blue, and at the last, huge red, white, and blue. That burst filled the sky, an umbrella descending in cascades around us, pulling us together in our tinyness huddled on the sand. I felt real joy.

And yet for Randy, just home from the Gulf War, the detonations brought back horror, the streaks across the sky the announcement of destruction.

Life is mixed, we say. It's always mixed. Sometimes the messenger comes to say we've won the sweepstakes. Sometimes it is the news of death.

Breaking in can bring harm. An old woman lived beneath us back in our law school days. Before she moved into that apartment, two women lived there who worked for the phone company by day, and were prostitutes at night who probably sold drugs. The news that they had left did not get all the way around. In the middle of the night great trucks, eighteen wheelers, would pull up in the parking lot. Drunken drivers would lurch out and come pounding on the door of the old woman. She was very frail and utterly refined. Her husband had been a small town minister. We would get up and go down and explain to the men that the other tenants had moved, but sometimes, if they were drunk enough, they would try to break down the door and see. Our poor neighbor would cower in her bed. It is an image of menace I've remembered ever since. Harm trying to break in.

Once, long ago, Randy ran through the sliding glass door that led out onto the porch. The kids were playing back there, clowning and dancing to loud music. When Randy left to answer the phone, they closed the door to keep the music from bringing me to insist they turn it down. He did not realize they had closed the door, and, in great high spirits, he jogged back out and struck it at full run. The sound of that great splintering is with me still. Horror sometimes crashes in on our world.

How can we understand suffering? There are so many kinds of hurt. I think about my mom. At eighty-one, she is in pain most of the time she is awake. "Old age is not for sissies," she observes. "It takes so much courage just to take a bath. To face the risk of falling. I give myself a medal when I do."

My dad is just fine physically. You would guess him to be two decades younger than he is. But his mind's confused.

His past keeps overtaking his present and he forgets the simplest things. He might get mad, and in the midst of putting forth his argument, forget what angered him. He can't be independent. He must be watched like a young child. Once he was the Chief of his Corps, the Judge Advocate General's Corps, the legal branch of the Army.

One of my best friends growing up has had tragic hardships. Her husband discovered on their honeymoon that he had Parkinson's disease. He died slowly and horribly over the next five years, leaving her with four small children. Both sons had damage to their brains from RH factor incompatibility. It is something that can now be prevented. Her freckled face is lined, arthritis swells her lovely hands. She has never lost her sense of wonder or gratitude or humor, but her pain has been enormous.

Someone I love very much battles mental illness. Manic-depressive is the diagnosis most often given. It is an agony, the imbalance stalking her, lurking, snarling, like all our deepest fears; the terrorizing, bottomless brutality of the agitated depression, and the alternating unremitting intensity of manic light where she cannot sleep or even rest.

Rejection is another form of suffering. A friend described what happened in this way. During the news one night, as casually as if she asked him for the paper, his wife informed him that she wanted him to leave. "I do not love you, and I haven't for some years. Now that the youngest is in college, I want you to move out. Be gone by morning."

Losing someone you love, however it happens, can unleash a pain that seems to take up the entire world. It's as if you cannot find a corner in yourself to stand and try to bear it. It is not really a shattering. That implies an event too quickly over. It is a slow, sickening wrench of the sinews of your being. The psychological term is de-cathecting. That is such an antiseptic word for the long, slow anguish of trying to reconstruct the center of your being.

There are so many kinds of suffering. I am trying to reflect here on the pain that is an inevitable part of life, the difficulties involved in living out our lives. It is important to me to be clear that pain is not something we should seek. Pain is an evil. It is not something to exult in. It is not holy to inflict pain upon ourselves. Self-inflicted suffering is never life-giving.

In situations where we once saw people (or ourselves) as "heroic martyrs" or "helpless, saintly victims" we now question whether there is "co-dependency." Is the person cooperating in their own abusing? Self-imposed anguish is *not* a virtue. God does not glory in our pain.

How do we enter the mystery of suffering? How can it be a place with some potential to meet love, not to wall love out? I have no final answers. This question was old when Job was on the dung heap. I just have some reflections, some observations from my own life and the lives of those who have let me know this part of them.

It is important to me that you view these conclusions as very humble offerings. The world of suffering is vast: hunger, poverty, oppression, disease, rank fear, desperate heartbreak. Some kinds of pain do not let up; people can twist and break and lose all life that seems worth living. These thoughts that have helped me may not help someone else. I only offer what has brought me life.

Goethe said that colors are the deeds and sufferings of light. I have found that sometimes colors can be prismed through the pain.

A great potential lies in the fact that suffering makes us vulnerable. We are broken open by it, we need help, we know that we need love. Theologians call it a *limit experience* in which we are forced to reach out of ourselves for help and meaning. For me it is the implication of the beatitudes. Blessed are we when we know we don't have it all together, for then we let in love.

It is the paradox of Paul's second letter to the Corinthians: "It is when I am weak that I am strong." Pushed to our limits, over our heads, we have to reach out. We have to grasp for power beyond us, we are forced into realizing dependence, we are pushed to risk discovering the enormous underpinnings of love. "My grace is enough for you, for in weakness my power reaches perfection" (2 Cor 12:9-10, *JB*).

What about people who do not find God's power in their weakness? What about those who reach out, and fall into a void of meaning? I do not know. I have no answer. Our old image of the tapestry where we see just the threads and knots, and God sees the pattern from the other side, is little consolation for those moments. My hope is that a time will come when love is felt and meaning shows itself from long perspective. The psalms are filled with lines that cry, "How long, O God, how long?" It is an ancient plaint. I cling to a hope that somehow, in our weakness, love will come.

There is a terrible story about a woman who works in my sister Peggy's office. I have never been able to tell it because it is so dreadful, but at the same time so enormously profound. The woman has begun to tell it herself to people whom it might help, support groups for people with similar experiences.

The woman is a mid-life person who became blind when she was twenty-one, already a mother. When we met I was deeply moved by her. She stood with her curling auburn hair and flowered dress, a great blonde guide dog by her side. There was a peace in her, a stillness and a power. I treasured the conversation we exchanged. A few months later my sister told me the awful news. The city paper had done a feature on this woman, describing her heroic life, raising her five boys after her divorce, working in a profession that cared for the aging. They had a picture of her with her children and her dog, and they printed where she lived.

Someone read that paper and began to follow her. He memorized her movements and watched who came and went into her house. One night when she was home alone he broke in through a basement window. She awoke to a noise; he grabbed her, put a knife to her throat and said he was going to kill her if she did not stop fighting him. He also told her he would kill her guide dog. He raped her more than once, and told her he knew where she lived and would come back to kill her if she told anyone. He left.

She called 911 and made it to the hospital. Her former husband was called to the emergency room. He kept the children for a few weeks. She said later to my sister that the experience had made her vulnerable. "I have tried so hard to be independent in my life," she said. "I was determined not to need anyone. When this happened, I couldn't help myself. I found out how much people loved me. I let them give to me. As strange as it seems, this incident showed me love. I felt *held* by God."

Suffering, as it throws us on our limits, can open us to love.

Knowing we are not alone in it may help most in our suffering. Years ago I had surgery. I didn't think it would be bad. (That just tells you I had never had surgery before.) My dear friend Benni insisted on coming with me even though it was in another town. She sat with me that morning. We talked and prayed together. She let me babble on and on when I'd had the pre-op shot. Afterwards she was there when I woke up. An old woman was in the other bed in my room, a backwoods cracker woman who looked as if she'd worked hard all her life. She was very frightened being there. She had not even gone to hospitals for childbirth.

"That must be your sister," she said to me. Benni and I looked at each other, considering. "Yes, you know, she is." We realize in a special way that we are brothers and sisters in times of pain.

"I'm glad you're both in here with me," she said. "It makes this seem a kinder place."

The first time I had this type of experience was when I had my first baby. I had prepared for that labor. I was going to offer the first twenty minutes for the souls in purgatory and the next twenty minutes for those imprisoned for the faith in China—I had a whole long list. I managed for about half an hour before the pain overtook me.

It is important to know that when pain is intense we get really lost in it. That is nothing to be ashamed of. It is crucial not to turn on ourselves because of that. Jesus himself cried out: "My God, my God why have you forsaken me?"

At times in that first labor I felt totally alone. But when the pains would ebb, I had a remarkable experience of not being alone. I was at an Army hospital at Ft. Bragg, N.C., a post with thousands of young couples who all seemed to be child-bearing. The labor and delivery section was jammed and very understaffed. I did not see a nurse for hours.

In the labor room with me toward the end (two other women had come and gone) was a black woman. She was having her fifth. She had four girls. She said, "This is your first, isn't it honey? And you're a long way from home."

She said it with real tenderness. She was much more concerned about me than she was about herself. She kept telling me how to breathe and push, kept telling me how well I was doing.

At one point she said, "Now honey, I'll be gone a minute, but I'll be back." She was gone about half an hour and then back. She'd had her baby! "Praise God, a fine strong boy!" she said. "Now how's your's coming?"

She insisted that they let her stay to help me until they took me to delivery. "You let me help this child, she needs me." About an hour later I had a daughter, delicate and lovely, dark-haired and strong. Every year on her birthday I think about that woman, give thanks for her, ask blessings on her son. She was my sister. She helped me in my pain. She was a corporal's wife, I was the wife of a West Point lieutenant. Her father was a Carolina cotton picker. I was a general's daughter. She gave to me. I was frightened and in the great poverty of ignorance and pain. She had the riches of experience, and an enormous heart.

Someone being with us helps us enter the mystery of suffering.

Most basic of all is that God is with us in it. Sometimes we lose that. We are still haunted by what most disturbed Job, that somehow suffering is a sign of God's disfavor. Job's friends kept saying "You must have sinned." We have a primitive image of God handing out the pain.

I think we must work to be grounded in the opposite reality. The God whom our scriptures bear witness to is a crucified God, no stranger to our suffering. God has not remained on the other side of pain, but has joined us on this side of human anguish. With God on the same side of suffering with us, it cannot swallow us up forever.

Some time ago, while I was home on vacation, a major crisis blew up. I was outraged. Not another crisis! Not on my vacation! I went for a walk in the woods by myself and ended up shouting to the sky: "I do not need another rotten opportunity for greatness!"

Gently, sadly, it was as if I heard replied: "Neither do I! How are we going to get each other through this one?"

We are not alone.

Somehow suffering has meaning. There is no way to prove this, or even explain it, and, I don't know, it might not even be true of all suffering. All we can do is leap to our faith in what we call the paschal mystery itself.

Death led to life.

Crucifixion was followed by resurrection.

Somehow the grain of wheat falls to the ground and dies, and *then* it bears its fruit.

The fruit I have noticed most of all in people who have suffered is the birth of compassion. Leon Bloy wrote in "Love Suffers" that "We have places in our hearts which do not yet exist, and into them we enter suffering in order that they may have existence."

Kim, the daughter of my friend Benni, was in an accident this winter. She was taking pictures, I think for the yearbook, sitting on the hood of a car. The car was going very slowly, but somehow she fell and it ran over her. They tried to back it off, and only dragged her underneath. Her leg was broken in four places, and she had third degree burns from being up against the catalytic converter. The burns were terrible to heal. The doctors tried not to do a skin graft, not wanting to scar her further by taking other skin. What she went through those weeks of scraping, soaking, and breaking open could not be put in words. The responses of the nurses, Benni related to me later, was notable. Some said: "Don't act like a baby, straighten up!" when Kim would writhe and cry and find it more than she could bear.

This young woman is a *trooper*, she was brave and stoic way beyond her years. But burns are dreadful, and they were not healing, only getting worse. The nurse who really helped her was one who'd been in pain herself. She didn't pass it off as "just discomfort." "You feel like you won't make it one more hour," she said, "I know. I know." Compassion is forged from having been there on your way.

I remember a group of us at Ft. Bragg—eight lieutenants' wives—many of our husbands from the same West Point class. Each woman had a certain look after her baby came. It was after the experience of pregnancy, labor, and delivery, and then those first hard weeks of being up at night, of being so unsure of what the crying meant, of not knowing how to ever do it all. I remember noticing it in Joan. She was the first of us to go through it. I said to myself: "She looks like she has been through the fire." She seemed taller, more beautiful, more humble, more—well—real. She said: "There is very little time for personal loveliness!" But she was lovelier.

I think it is very, very important, at least nothing has ever been more important for me in bearing suffering, physical or psychological, than knowing that somehow it is part of the paschal mystery. That there will be life on the other side of this; *more* life. Without it, the grain of wheat remains alone, the gospel says. The falling to the ground, the dying, brings the fruit.

Jesus was not the same when he rose from the dead. His was not just a resuscitated body, like the body of Lazarus unwrapping from the tomb. Jesus was different. Those who saw him did not recognize him. Over and over in the appearance stories this was the case. He did not look the same. He was transformed. Somehow, in our sufferings, so are we.

In some cases, the people who saw him—the women and the disciples—thought he was a ghost, that he was from another world. He insisted that they touch him and he shared their food. He was alive *here*, in this world, transformed, but very real. He still had the marks of his wounds. *Our* wounds are part of transformation.

Knowing our lives are one with the dying and rising of Jesus can help so much. It may be the central lesson of the heart. Sometimes we may have a moment to pass it on to someone who has not yet quite realized it. The opportunity is very delicate. It could sound like moralizing, like trivializing another person's pain. "Oh, good for you, another chance to be transformed!"But sometimes making the connection can be a gift. You've probably done it many times. I remember once for me.

It happened on the phone. I had a call, mid-week, mid-morning, from a woman I had not heard from in over fifteen years. I had been on her mind a lot, she said, and she just decided to see if she could find me and discover how the years had treated me. I was scrubbing the kitchen floor when she tracked me down, and when I told her that, we both laughed. We had just hated scrubbing floors when we knew each other years before.

We had met in the Army Post at a coffee for officers' wives. Our husbands were newly stationed there. We were standing next to each other in line, and found out in a few minutes that both our names were Pat, both of us were expecting babies at the same time, and both of us were Catholic. We formed a bond that day that kept us close the whole time of that station.

We lost touch somehow after that, but every Easter I thought of her because she had made darling tiny baskets for my children that I always used as a centerpiece for Easter dinner. Now, on the phone, we talked of many things, my brush and bucket quite forgotten. She caught me up on all four of her children in some headlines, and I did the same with mine.

Then she went back to Joe. Joe was their oldest, perhaps the brightest, handsomest. She told how after years and years of crises, doctors were finally sure he was manic-depressive. They were treating him with lithium, and the disorder seemed under control. He had a job, was living on his own, stable and happy. "I am so grateful," she said. "There has been so much pain."Deeply moved, remembering Joe well, a captivating tow-head, I said, almost to myself: "It's the paschal mystery."

"What?" she asked.

"The dying and rising."

There was a silence. And then, "It is. It *is*!"

I wish you could have heard Pat's voice. Pat is the salt-of-the-earth, utterly dependable, capable embodiment of hearth and home and country. She chose 1776 for their mail-box number, and led the family rosary if she could ever round the others up.

What had been missing for her was the symbol, the distillation of the truth that named her experience and let her claim its meaning. Year after year I'd had the little baskets, one with lace and ribbon and seed pearls, the other with brass buttons and red and blue velvet. (There were just two, Boo was not yet born.) I had her baskets in the middle of my Easter table, but she did not have all the truth connected inside of her.

"It is . . .": the truth connecting.

Her voice sounded as if something totally simple, yet utterly and fundamentally profound, had filled her whole world. Her voice was soft and bright, as if she were seeing some kind of dawn. All the fear and anguish, the shame and devastation, the police stations and hospitals and shipwrecks of hope suddenly fell into meaning. The terrifying landscape of night became in that sunrise a cross and an empty tomb.

"Peace be to you," she said. I couldn't tell if she said it to me, or was repeating it, hearing it back, spoken to herself.

"Peace," I said.

After a long, full silence, we both hung up.

Nothing has ever meant as much to me as learning that all the heartbreak and failure, all the weakness and the death of dreams, all the shapes and textures and colors and sounds of a thousand lettings-go, were the paschal mystery.

To pass that on to my friend, to have that mean something to her, was one of the beautiful moments of my life. The water in my scrub bucket had gotten cold. As I emptied it to start again with hot water, I felt the wonder. This is holy ground. When we enter the mystery of suffering we are somehow on holy ground.

Moving into suffering, the change from light to dark, the falling to the ground of the grain of wheat, is the theme of the Bible. No character escapes this rhythm: not Abraham or David, Ruth or Mary, the Magdalene or Paul.

Demetrius Dumm, a marvelous Benedictine theologian, teaches biblical spirituality for our program. He calls this "the genetic code of the Bible": first we know God's love through ways we understand. God speaks to us in our language. We learn to trust. We know God's care, God's tenderness, God's present love. Demetrius leans forward on the podium, a twinkle in his eye. "And then . . . and then God gets mysterious," he says.

"This is the whole theme of the Bible," he explains. "It is *everywhere*. It is the meaning of God's name."[1]

Somehow challenge and suffering are how we grow up. They are the fire, the hammer blows, that form us on a forge. They call out the strengths that would have gone unformed. "God loves us too much to allow us to remain children," Demetrius says. "God knows we need to be called to some things that are hard."

I found his explanation very confirming. I knew that was the story of my own life, but I didn't realize it was everybody's life, that all of scripture had this theme, that it is the genetic code of the Bible. When Demetrius Dumm pointed to it, I could certainly see it was the history of the Jews, a history of triumph and trial, of prosperity and total loss. They were conquered by the Assyrians, probably the most dreaded enemy in all of history, and either scattered or destroyed or taken prisoner to Babylon. Gone was their temple, their language, their royal line, forever. It was during that captivity, expressed in the writings of Second Isaiah, that the realization came to them: success and wealth are not the signs of God's favor. God cannot save us from physical destruction, but God will never leave us. "Do not be afraid, for I am with you and I love you." "I have carved your name on the palm of my hand" (cf. Is 43:2-5; 49:16).

Both Old and New Testaments tell these stories. The genetic code in the lives of the ancient biblical men and women was most fully true in the life of Jesus. At first there were clear signs of the presence of God, and then there was mysterious challenge. First there were times of miracles and crowds of thousands. Then he moved to Jerusalem and Gethsemane and death.

Can't pain be prevented? Why couldn't God protect us? Doesn't it say in Luke "I have given you power to tread down serpents and scorpions . . . nothing shall ever hurt you" (Lk 10:19)? I heard master storyteller and theologian John Shea speak on this passage. "We need to consider," he said wryly, "what harm meant to Jesus. Reflect on how he ended up! Harm did not mean to him what it means to us. For Jesus, the deepest harm is breaking of relationship, the double relationship of God and neighbor. That is real harm."

The assurance we have from God is that the relationship will hold. God will be with us with sustaining love. If that is true, nothing can really destroy us. Somehow, *somehow*, even though it is beyond our understanding, perhaps even beyond the bounds of this lifetime, we will bear fruit. There will be a way we might not know until death in which we will be transformed into love by the God who was holding us through it all.

Years ago I read a biography of seventeenth-century poet John Donne. There was a powerful description of the death of his wife, Anne. She was delirious with fever, and kept calling and calling for him. She could not tell in her terrible torment that he was right beside her, holding her, answering.

Even if we can trust that God is somehow with us, how do we stand the pain? Anyone who has ever really suffered knows that question is quite just. Kim (my friend's daughter who got run over by the car), before they finally gave in and did a skin graft on her burns, had days and nights she was sure she could not bear it. Somehow we try to just endure.

"How will I ever do it?" I have moaned, when some big challenge fell again.

"The same way I did it before, I guess," I try to answer to myself. "The same way I cleaned up forty-eight ounces of cooking oil spilled by the baby on the kitchen floor twenty minutes before a dinner party. The same way I drove one hundred miles each way for every class of graduate school. You don't do it all at once. Just the next task. Just this five minutes."

My friend Frank McNulty tells the story of Janet Lynn, the skater. She always performed, he recounts, in the shadow of other great women skaters. The frequent refrain was, "She's good, but not as good as (for example) Peggy Fleming." Despite this, Janet started to get ready for the Olympics with all she had. She got up early, and practiced late, a grinding, constant routine. Finally she was ready. This was her chance. The big day came, she was out on the ice, doing her beautiful routine to music. Four minutes into it, she slipped and fell in a wet spot on the ice. Even so, her performance was still good enough to get the bronze medal. Without the fall, she clearly had the gold. Afterwards, she was mobbed by reporters, trying to outshout each other to get her attention. One finally could be heard above the rest: "What did you think about when you fell?" She gave him that look that young people can give, puzzled at absurdity. "I thought about getting up."

We work at getting up. We move the next step. And we try to believe it has meaning. We try not to give in to despair and cynicism, although it seems quite tempting. (It's hard, sometimes, not to sing the refrain of a country song I heard once that said: "Work your fingers to the bone, and what do you get? Bony fingers. Bony fingers.")

There are seasons of these challenges or sufferings in all our lives. Physical pain comes sometimes—breaks or sprains or illnesses, kidney stones or migraines. Or it can be anguish of the spirit: losses or depression—"the mean reds," Holly-Go-Lightly calls them in *Breakfast at Tiffany's*. Failures, disillusions, rejections that fill us with the aching sense of the song "When the Shadows Came to Stay." There can be the devouring angst that someone we love is in trouble or in danger. Or, worst of all, the Ogre.

Elizabeth Goudge, my favorite English novelist, wrestles with this mystery in her books. Like any of us, she could not explain it, but she helps us see how we might embrace it.

In *The Heart of the Family* she has Hilary, the endearing, unpretentious Vicar, speak about it. He is often tormented at night by his fears and guilts.

> For there is always the Thing, you know, the hidden Thing, some fear or pain or shame, temptation or bit of self-knowledge that you can never explain to another . . . if you just endure it simply because you must, like a boil on the neck, or fret yourself to pieces trying to get rid of it, or cadge sympathy for it, then it can break you. But if you accept it as a secret borne secretly for the love of Christ, it can become your hidden treasure. For it is your point of contact with him, your point of contact with that fountain of refreshment down at the roots of things. "O Lord, thou fountain of living waters."
>
> That fountain of life is what Christians mean by grace. That is all. Nothing new, for it brings us back to where we were before. In those deep green pastures where cool waters are there is no separation. Our point of contact with the suffering Christ is our point of contact with

> every other suffering man and woman, and is the source of life.[2]

I have thought of this so often in times of pain or fear. When I am very worried about money, I am aware of the multitude of parents, most of the world, who have no sure way to feed their children, for whom never knowing if they can survive is a constant way of life. We are one in the human condition, I tell myself, and try to picture all of us by the fountain of living waters.

How does suffering occur? This is the puzzle we will never untangle. How could God allow it? Does God cause it? How could God be all-powerful if . . . ? We'll never figure it out. The best that we can do is try to enter trusting.

We try to trust, we try to endure. Sometimes there is strength in what my sister Peg calls "the remembering trick"—remembering other hard times we have survived. We can recall the feeling then that we didn't know how we would make it, and also the fact that somehow we did.

Sometimes practical things can help us endure, like scrubbing the kitchen or cleaning out the garage. Sometimes it helps to buy a bunch of flowers or get ten books out of the library or take the time to eat. For me it is important not to eat watching or reading the news. There is so much tragedy in the news.

It helps to look at Jesus' life. The scripture says "the Spirit *drove* him into the desert and he remained there for forty days, and was put to the test by Satan" (Mk 1:12). Forty days and forty nights Jesus struggled. This was right after the baptism, the pinnacle moment of the Father's speaking: "You are my Son, the Beloved; my favor rests on you" (vs. 11). The very next passage is the desert.

We, too, are lured into the desert. "To make our souls," the English say. In the trial, we find out who we are. The times of these are intermittent. They are cycles, Ignatius says, of consolation and desolation. The truth of this is very, very old. The Psalms, sung by heart hundreds of years before Jesus learned to sing them, tell of this:

Those that sow in tears
  shall reap rejoicing.

Although they go forth weeping,
  carrying the seed to be sown,
They shall come back rejoicing,
  carrying their sheaves (Ps 126:5-6, *NAB*).

We could never make it through if this weren't so. It is horrible to think of there not being any rest. After Randy ran through the glass door, his arm and leg and chin all cut wide open, there were hundreds of stitches and weeks of recuperation. But then he moved, scarred but healthy, into many years of strength.

Each time we are caught up in a time of struggle ("Boot camp, again," my friends and I say) we go into the dark. What rising comes is always on the other side. There's no short cut. We have to let go, accept the fact that the falling to the ground is here again. It is the Gethsemane time. Demetrius Dumm says that the Garden was the worst of Jesus' Passion: the struggling to avoid it, the desperation not to drink the cup. Perhaps that's true for us each time as well. The hardest part is to let go, to trust. I have a friend in the midst of the anguish of a divorce after twenty-five years. He feels as if he may never be free of pain again. He repeats to himself the lines from Robert Frost:

Yet all the precedent is on my side.
I know that winter death has never tried
The earth, but it has failed.[3]

On the other side of dying, some new life begins. Scripture scholar Don Senior preached for us at liturgy when he last came to teach in our program. He spoke softly, almost tenderly, of something he had noticed. The moments of dying are often loud and harsh and public in our lives. The wrenching fills the world. In contrast, the risings are mostly quite simple. One day the pain has lessened. A tree blooms out of season. We find we are able to sleep. Someone we pass on the street looks at us and smiles, and we find ourselves smiling.

In the hard times we think that no good thing can happen out of all of the difficulty. But then, imperceptibly at first, some good makes a small beginning.

"My barn having burned to the ground, I can now see the moon," a friend quoted from a Chinese proverb. She said it slowly, looking at her hands. She had been speaking of the terribly difficult season the last few years had been for her. First there had been an enormous professional disappointment, a clear injustice, that devastated her and left her without a job. Then, a personal loss, the ending of the relationship that had been central in her life. "I thought the depression would never lift," she had been saying. "All I felt was loss. Last week someone sent me a card with the Chinese proverb.

"I knew what it meant to have my barn burned to the ground." There was pause, and then she looked up, her blue eyes lit with a touch of wonder. "That same night, as I was going to bed, I went to the window. I realized that for the first time in a very long time I could see the moon."

9

We Need to Nurture Hope

One of the most significant lessons of the heart concerns hope. In these last few years I have come to know the gift of hope as central, a grace with power at the heart of life itself. This conviction has come to me in different ways, sometimes in vignettes.

One early summer I was in New York's La Guardia, an airport often choked and clogged even in smooth times. This particular week the area of my ticket counter was under construction. The line must have had thirty people in it, crammed and crowded with little visible movement forward as the departure times got closer.

Somewhat in front of me was a German family apparently in the U.S. to sightsee for a while. A couple and two daughters, all different shades of blond, all striking looking. The girls were bickering a little about who would get to sit on the large suitcase, both bored and tired in the endless line.

When the parents weren't looking, the younger one, who had just lost her place on the suitcase, ducked around me in line and took off. I was far enough back to see her going around the temporary wooden partition. I watched her wind around the stalls and shops and services that make modern airports more and more like medieval fairs. All of a sudden she stopped and looked around, and I could tell she was confused. The wooden partition hid her from her family.

She was about thirteen, a vulnerable age for asking assistance. To admit you are not in charge of things is terribly embarrassing. I had also gathered that she spoke no English. She looked around in a kind of searching panic.

Just then her father, who had been looking for her, came around the corner.

"Papa!"

He was very tall and lean, his hair a kind of red gold. "Liebchen," he said, and gathered her to him, her head not reaching his chin. He stroked her hair, and ran the back of his hand down her cheek. Then he gave a little twitch on the braid down her back, and stepped away. He put on a very serious scowl, and said some fierce guttural sentences which I assumed in the universal language of parents was: "You stay with us every single minute, as we have told you over and over and over again!"

They both burst out laughing. With their arms around each other they went back in line with the mother and the sister.

Maybe it was because I was very tired that day, my energy low and flat, that the current of their exchange came rushing through me with such force. What I felt was *hope*. When we get lost, when we are no longer in charge, when we can't seem to speak the language of a situation, sometimes we experience the presence of love. A love that seems to hold us, and smooth our hair, and run a hand along our cheek. A love that laughs great dancing laughter after scolding.

I wanted them to be on my flight. I thought it might be possible, since I was going to Orlando, and Disney World is often the first stop most tourists want to make. They were not with me. Maybe it was just as well. None of us can stand observing in our interactions for too long. They had a right to their privacy, to some possible interludes of crankiness. I wanted to hang on to my hope.

These last years I have been pleading a case within myself for hanging on to hope. It is so important. I don't think we talk enough about hope.

Last year there was a priest in our program who came from the tribal area of Bangladesh. He said hope drew the natives there to Christianity. He said they were amazed by it. Love they found natural. In every tribe they knew, people loved their own. Faith they found expectable. Faith in some kind of deity sprang up in different forms in every people that they knew. But what Christianity offered, what did not seem natural to them, what puzzled and excited and finally converted them was that the sign of this Christian God was hope. To have hope there must be a God, they told him.

I don't think we reflect much on the fundamental place of hope. I don't think—at least I haven't in my life—we nurture hope the way we nurture faith and love.

We know we need to nurture faith. We spend time and energy on liturgy and scripture, on reading and prayer, on talking to other people about God's presence in our lives.

We know we need to nurture love. Married love, for example, must be cultivated. Married couples discover they just can't assume that their love will bloom forever. Life is very hard. Illnesses and difficult moments with children and jobs, jealousies and differences and limits of all kinds, strain the love. Couples learn that they must create moments for conversations and special times and thoughtfulness and honesty and unselfishness and humor if the love is to survive and strengthen.

A friend of mine called not long ago to read me a note her husband had put for her on top of the leftover pot roast. It said: "This pot roast is better the second time and the third. So are we. Good thing we will last a lot longer than the pot roast. Especially since I am taking most of it for lunch. Hope you weren't planning to have it for supper!"

Faith matures when we care for it. Love deepens and grows both more fruitful and more comfortable. And so it is with hope. But if we do not nurture it, it can be choked out before it has a chance to mature.

In love, we try to give the other person the benefit of the doubt. We consciously try to remember their strengths, we try not to hoard slights and concentrate on every resentment.

This is just as important in hope. It is imperative not to pore over every disappointment and magnify every anxiety. Instead, we need to let the graces sing their plainchant, and shine the spotlight on the times—despite all odds—we made it to safety.

I find I have to *work* at this. What seems more natural is to focus on the fears. To scan the past for what went wrong, and face the future expecting trouble. How often casual get-togethers—at the office having lunch, in the front yard at the mail box—turn into an exchange of what is wrong. Wrong with the weather, for starters, with the world, with kids today, with prices at the grocery store, with all of it.

I am really becoming aware that this is a harmful thing, at least for me. It may be a way to let off steam. It also lets in cynicism and fear.

Perhaps because the last few years have been years of tremendous transition for me, I have been acutely aware of my own vulnerability. Because there have been major crises in every generation of my family, I have begun to see that it is not a minor thing being careless about hope. How can hope be expected to gather strength and resilience when I assault it thoughtlessly over and over? It is like belittling love with sarcasm and intolerance, for focusing on the slightest failing.

When I began to realize this, I started to pay attention to what I did to undermine hope. Then I tried to notice what seemed to encourage its life. I have come to believe that we have a serious and central obligation to put ourselves in the presence of beauty, within earshot of truth, within the touch of goodness. We need to open the windows and doorways to these signs of God's life, for they are sources of hope.

I discovered this during one very stressful time when I was about as worn out as I have gotten. I had the new full-time position with the renewal program, but was still sandwiching in talks planned before I took the job. I had just finished two days of a demanding workshop in Washington, and faced getting home very late, and having to go to work in early morning. I could hardly stand to think about not getting any time to rest. An old friend was driving me to the airport. Instead of taking me to lunch, which had been the plan, she brought cheese and fruit and checkered napkins in the car and stopped at the National Gallery of Art.

"This will do you much more good," she said as we pulled up by the museum. We walked through the archways of that magnificent foyer past the statue of Mercury into an exhibit of Georgia O'Keeffe. I had thought Georgia did mostly cow skulls. There were rooms of flowers and skies and mountains and trees; incredible colors, mind-stretching perspectives. When I got on the plane, I felt more alive than I had in weeks. That was when I began to realize that beauty can bring us to hope.

We can't always get to a gallery. I began to find that beauty within easy reach could sometimes do it too. The color of the edge of daffodils. The shape of flaming leaves on a downdraft of the autumn wind. Bird song on the turn of dawn and on the turn of dark.

Hope is not the naive expectation that all will go smoothly, that desolation will remain a stranger. It is a conviction that God will always be with us in whatever happens. That sounds like the most obvious spiritual cliché. It is just a cliché until something happens that disturbs our world.

I learned that in my transition. I didn't expect it to be hard. I would be going back home at Christmas and in summers. I would be home when my youngest, the only one not completely out of the nest, was home from college. I was excited about the job, looking forward to a splendid person to work with, and to being part of an excellent organization. The football team looked like it had a good chance of being number one. I had a charming apartment over the garage of a lovely old home.

Besides . . . I had taught workshops in transition. I knew all about it. (It is a peculiar arrogance that thinks because you know about something you somehow won't be affected by it.)

Well, what happened was that I had a very intense sense of disorientation and disconnection. A classic identity crisis. Who was I here? What did it mean to be Associate Director? For ten years I had been free-lancing as a speaker. I had been at microphones in front of audiences. Suddenly I needed to know how the copier could collate. I was the one everyone asked where the extra toilet paper was kept. The worst part was, I didn't know.

And I was living alone. Somehow it was very different from being alone in my little house where the kids had grown up. Even when they left home for school or marriage or the military, it was as if their voices and footfalls were just out of hearing. Their books and trophies and records and fingerprints were still around. Their measurements on the broom closet door. Everything in this new apartment was just for me.

It really overwhelmed me the day I heard kids in the driveway talking. The family that lived in the main house had six kids. One of them had friends over. As I was unlocking my door after work, I heard one of them say: "Who is that?"

"Oh, that's nobody; just the lady over the garage," another boy replied.

When you move from being the mom to the lady over the garage, it is a major change. I sat that night for a long time in the quiet dark in a tide of what St. Ignatius calls desolation.

The very next week there came to teach in our program a scripture scholar from Catholic Theological Union named Dianne Bergant. She talked about Yahweh, the God of the Israelites, as the God of the dispossessed.

It was one of those times, as I sat in the back row among the forty-two priests participating that fall, that I knew I was hearing the key to the mystery. The God of the dispossessed. I felt a tangible surge of hope.

Our God is not a God who waits in the Promised Land. Yahweh is a God of the journey. A nomad God. A God who comes along in the unfamiliar. A God who can live over the garage.

I think it is very important to say quickly that Yahweh is not *only* a God of dispossession. Yahweh is also a God of our most poignant and powerful experiences of homecoming. A God who is also with us in the Promised Land, and who invented the idea of milk and honey.

But somehow it is the key to the mystery that real hope is not born until we feel ourselves struggle to keep from going under in the eddies of some loss.

Of course, this was not the first time I had experienced the painful way that real hope happens. It is strange, though, how each time it feels a little like the first time, a frightening unknown. But the first time is the hardest, certainly. We have no experience of coming out the other side.

I remember Kadee's first time. This happened when she was a freshman in college. When she went away, she left behind her on the family land Princess, the pony she had bought with all her money in the second grade. She bought her on the same day she made her first communion. I need to say, in all fairness, that she hadn't ridden or paid much attention to Princess in a while. Other things had become primary in her life.

It was expensive to feed Princess, to get her hoofs trimmed and give her shots. It was a lot of work to pump the water in her trough. No one rode her. When Kadee came home for vacation, she discovered that Princess had been sold to the horse dealer. Kadee went wild. She felt terrible grief. She just knew that Princess had probably gone to some dog-food factory. It really affected her deeply. The loss of Princess was also like the loss of her girlhood, the familiar beloved world.

A whole year later, by some fluke, she found out that Princess had not gone to the dog-food factory, but had been bought by a family with a little second grade girl. They had bred Princess to another pony, the first time she had been bred, and she had a foal.

We drove fifty miles to see her. What an experience! Not only was she not dead in some ignominious slaughter house, but she had given birth to new life. When we got along the side of the pasture, Kadee saw Princess out in the grass with a darling red-brown foal with a blonde mane and tail. "I'm a grandmother," she said softly.

We climbed through the barbed wire, and, as we approached, Princess gave a whinny and came right over and nuzzled Kadee. "She remembers!"

I have long heard it told that horses have no memory for anything but food, but I can say for sure that horse remembered. There was still loss. The pony belonged to the little girl. Kadee had to let her go. But also, in some way, she got her back. The next Easter, as Kadee and I sat listening to the reading of the resurrection, she leaned over to me and said, "Like Princess." That story is a foundation for her hope.

Times of difficulty are important. In those moments of dispossession we know that we need saving. Not saving from sin, as we have often narrowly thought of salvation, but saving from being crushed. We can crush so easily. We can be utterly vulnerable, broken open, unmoored, unable to control. In that moment we are wide open to God's saving love which can gather us up and bring us to peace.

A great friend of mine had a heart attack not long ago, a triple by-pass with lots of complications that brought slow, disheartening recovery. When I say peace, I think of what he said one day.

"People get the wrong idea about peace," he said. "It is not cool and blue."

I know what he means. Peace is not the total absence of struggle. It is knowing we are not alone in it. It is having a trust—what Gabriel Marcel calls the shining of that veiled, mysterious light—that somehow, on some level, all will be well.

My favorite saying is from Julian of Norwich, that amazing woman of wisdom, a contemporary of Plantagenet kings, who lived in times of unimaginable turmoil just after the Black Death. She wrote in *The Revelations of Divine Love* that "All shall be well, and all shall be well, and all manner of thing shall be well."

That is the core of hope. But hope does not just happen. We have to work on it. I am trying to catch myself doing what Eric Berne, M.D. (author of *Games People Play*) calls "Ain't it Awful." I am trying to blow the whistle on myself when I am dredging up all that could possibly worry me. I was challenged on this once by a friend.

It was several summers ago. My parents lived in San Diego, a continent away from us three daughters scattered in the east. We had a bargain with one of their neighbors that if anything happened we needed to know about she would call us.

She called me one morning saying mom was sick. It was nothing serious, but it worried my dad so much, with his diminished ability to understand, that he was really vulnerable. When mom would fall asleep, he would get very frightened, and wake her up to be sure she was all right. The neighbor was calling to say mom was getting much worse because she couldn't rest, and one of us should come. Then dad could relax.

I was the most free to go. My one commitment was to meet with the head of a separated and divorced group in Miami who was planning a workshop. He was a friend, and I asked him to meet me at the airport there. I would drive the three hours to Miami and just fly from there.

As I was leaving the house it was raining hard, and I was horrified to notice that my roof was leaking. Water was coming through the ceiling close to the sliding glass door. I tried to put a bucket there, but the drip was too close to the door. No bucket was narrow enough. It is a terrible risk to leave your house in Florida in hurricane season with a leaking roof. You could come home to find everything afloat. I settled on the solution of taking the biggest, strongest garbage bag I had and fastening it to the ceiling around the leak with air-conditioning duct tape. I made three rows of tape, then blessed it, and walked out.

I drove through the Everglades to Miami, met my friend, worked out the design for the workshop. Then he asked me about my trip. I told him I was terribly worried. I mentioned first of all, that I thought dad would meet me, but I knew he wouldn't be able to find the car in the parking lot. It wasn't that he couldn't find it that concerned me (I often can't find mine), it was how he feels about himself when he can't find it. And even if he finds the car, sometimes he can't remember where he put the ticket to get out. I talked about my anxiety about my father first. Then I expressed my fear about my mom, what might be wrong.

Before I could go on, my friend interrupted me to say: "You know what I hate about you, Pat?"

This is not my favorite introduction to a topic. I did not reply, just looked at him.

"You're always dreading things," he said. "Last year you had a family reunion. Before you left, all you could talk about was what might go wrong. It would probably rain. The cousins wouldn't like each other. Your kids would act like they never used indoor plumbing, or hold up the cloth napkins at the dinner and say 'What's that?' When you came home you said it was the best exchange your family ever had. It makes me sick. I worry about you, and things turn out fine. I hate the way you dread things."

I was incensed. How dare he! I was the most positive person I knew. The nerve! They called my flight as I muttered something bitterly, like "Thank you for helping me grow."

As I was boarding, walking down the jetway, he called after me: "Livingston! Look for the surprises!"

I was mortified. Even the pilot looked at me as I got on. I was angry all the way to San Diego. As we were flying in, the plane swung out over the ocean to turn around and land. The sun was setting. The whole world was aflame with brightness, the sea a perfect mirror for the sky. I caught my breath. Then something in me said "Wait a minute. This is not surprising. I am not surprised. The sun always sets in the west!"

But as the time went on, one thing after another caused me wonder. Dad was right there at the gate with a great hug. He walked straight to the car in the parking lot. The next morning a lark sang me awake. I didn't even know there were larks in California. And mom got better right away. With rest and company she quickly healed. An uncanny thing happened one day. She came in to my room and said, out of the blue, "How's your roof? I've been thinking about your house. It is almost twenty years old, and it has never had the roof replaced." I started to demur, but she gave me a look that said, "I'll know the truth."

"Well, as a matter of fact, it's leaking."

"You left your roof leaking in hurricane season?"

So, I explained about the garbage bag, about the duct tape, about the blessing. She left the room and came back with a check book. She wrote a check and tore it off and gave it to me: a check for a new roof. My parents do not have a lot of money. What they have they're saving for doctors' bills and nursing homes, not wanting to be a burden on us. A roof is major money. There was the check right in my hand.

"Oh, Mom, this is incredibly generous," I said. I was too moved to get any other words out. Inside myself I fought with the admission: this was a very surprising event.

The last night I was there she and dad and I were sitting on the balcony of their apartment. Off in the distance we could see the ocean. Again the sun was setting: gold and crimson and pale, pale pink. We watched it deepen into rose, and saw the evening star appear, low and alive. Moved by that, at the same time, they began to recite Tennyson's poem "Crossing the Bar." This wasn't surprising for dad—he recites Shakespeare to the woman at the check-out counter—

but it was for mom. She has a kind of careful reserve. But she spoke it, too:

Sunset and evening star
  And one clear call for me!
May there be no moaning of the bar
  When I put out to sea,

They kept on through the verses until:

Twilight and evening bell,
  And after that the dark!
And may there be no sadness of farewell,
  When I embark.

I sat there in that pink-edged dusk with tears coming down my face. I did not say I was not surprised. I was overwhelmed with gratitude for these beautiful gutsy people who had given me birth.

When I flew home the next day, I was hoping my friend would not remember when I was due to return. I did not want to have to admit that he had been right. But when I got off the plane, there he was. I blushed and said "You were right. I was surprised. I was."

He had the decency not to gloat. (Which just tells you that I had been *dreading* that he would gloat. You don't get over it all at once.)

The kind of perspective he had challenged me to requires a shift in thought, a reversal. It reminds me of a wonderful thing Demetrius Dumm said in his class. He talked about David as a man of hope. He looked out at Goliath coming at him across the battlefield, and he did not say: "He is so big, how can I defeat him?" Instead he said: "He is so big, how can I miss him? What a target!" This shift does not come easily to most of us. We need to work on it.

The first thing that helps us with hope is: Don't open the door to needless anxiety. Try to stamp out the dread routine. The second thing is: See it as imperative to put ourselves in the presence of beauty and goodness and truth.

It is important to reflect on sources of beauty for each of us. I find that sunrise and sundown are times of magic. It is as if, when the light is angled with the change of day and night, there is a door open into All There Is.

There are many sources of beauty. On the Notre Dame campus there is a lovely art museum with a wing with the huge sculptures of Ivan Mestrovic that fill me with a sense of the stark and earthy power of the Good. Upstairs is hung Chagall's great canvas of the circus, all color, motion, playfulness.

Beauty is also in much more mundane places. I have a friend who practices what she calls "the aestheticism of the mall." She takes $2.50 and no credit cards and walks around malls looking at things she likes. I find malls quite overloading, but there is a shop I love in South Bend on the river called The Mole Hole. It has the most amazing things: kaleidoscopes and music boxes, merry-go-round horses and china clowns, crystal oil lamps and life-sized dolls. They don't mind if you just browse and I go every few weeks. It's important to think of places that have beauty for us.

Music is a doorway into hope. *Les Miserables* impacted me more than any music in my life. It is such a hymn to mercy and to love. The final words just set me weeping at the death of Jean Valjean: "To love another person is to see the face of God."

Lots of music stirs me: jazz and country, musicals and instrumentals. I was recently enchanted in an evening concert of Michael Feinstein playing Gershwin and Irving Berlin and great romantic music from over fifty years. When the audience poured out as it was over, our group, and then others as they saw us, began dancing up the street. Feinstein had connected us with something archetypal and beloved deep within.

I try to keep the music I like best from really wearing out. I put tapes away that really move me before I've gotten sick of them, saving them for those occasions when I need the door to open.

Truth is such a source of power: great passages from books and plays; poems read aloud. Books I love are many: Elizabeth Goudge's English novels, John Shea's poems and stories, Mary Stewart's tales of Merlin and Arthur, Ursula Le Guin's exquisite wizard books, the Earthsea trilogy. There are the children's stories like *The Secret Garden* and *The Wind in the Willows* and *Bridge Over Terebithia,* and, of course, C. S. Lewis' Narnia tales.

Splendid books are Peter Beagle's *The Last Unicorn,* John Knowles' *A Separate Peace,* and Olive Ann Burns' *Cold Sassy Tree.* All these books have parts to read aloud with joy. Reading aloud can be a strong support for hope. Sometimes I get together with a friend and we take turns. Favorite things we choose include Elise Maclay's poetry, *Green Winter,* and the provocative, whimsical *Book of Qualities* by J. Ruth Gendler (given to me by my friend Mary, who is the best person in the world for finding this kind of thing). Perhaps as I list these books I treasure, you will be thinking of sources like this for you.

I have a dream of having gatherings in my home called "Songs and Stories." I've done forms of it sometimes. I have the men and women in our program over each semester for high tea. I use my Aunt Dee's lovely silver service, and people recite passages from things they know by heart. (Aunt Dee, a wonderful, witty Irish woman whose love of literature is only surpassed by her love of parties, considers this a fine use of her silver service.) We have had glorious collections of recitations: Kilmer interspersed with Shakespeare, Dante after Liza Doolittle, Hopkins followed by a Tanzanian chant.

I think in modern times we've lost the strength of songs and stories sung and spoken to each other. For millennia tales were told and tunes were played at the ending of a day. It happened around campfires, in cottages, in great mead halls. VCRs and stereos are wonderful, but speaking aloud the words of truth to one another is a source of heartening we need.

Humor is as essential for hope as it is for mercy. Laughter has a goodness and a beauty far beyond expression. It comes from truth seen in perspective. It literally restores us physically, and it can give us back to ourselves inside.

"If there is a chance to do something fun, something refreshing, try to take it." This was advice given to me by Pauline, my wonderful neighbor across the street who helped me when my house flooded. Ten years ago when she and her husband moved here she confronted me. I had been telling her I felt badly that my yard was always such a mess. "I know it must bother you," I said.

"What bothers me," she answered, "is thinking you would worry about it bothering me. What I want is to know you're having fun. Don't waste your time while you are young slaving over some lawn. Don't wash windows when you could be visiting with a friend. Take every chance you get to relax and play. Your life is hard. Never work when you could be doing something wonderful because you think it bothers me! Take the chances that you get for fun." That has been very important for me through all these years.

I think there are three main secrets of supporting hope. The first I have described as avoiding anxiety if we can. Turn down the volume on dread. The second process is opening the doorways to beauty, truth, and goodness; songs and stories, laughter.

The third way to work on hope is replaying moments of life and love instead of reliving the times of pain. Retelling the stories, to ourselves and others, of moments of courage and surprise and glory can give real sustenance to hope. I will tell you two such stories I've tried to hang on to for myself.

The first happened in a recent May. My niece Liza graduated from college. It was Kenyon in central Ohio, a century-old jewel of liberal arts colleges.

Liza is a marvelous personage. She is tall, regal, statuesque. She has an arrestingly beautiful face, rose-cheeked and blue-eyed and fair, with tawny waist-length hair. She majored in music. When she opens her mouth, an incredible voice comes out, rich and true. She has not had an easy growing up. Brilliance in women of unconventional body types disconcerts the usual peer group.

I have loved Liza since she was born, just two weeks after my Boo. When they were both one (a year before the encounter with the wino in New Orleans) my sister came to visit. We were getting into the car; the garage was rather tight. The babies had to scoot over from the driver's side. Boo went in first. He paused behind the wheel, gripping it in both hands, saying loudly: "Beep, beep. Beep, beep." When Liza slid over she took the wheel as he had, but she said in her clear and lovely voice: "I am looking for a parking place." She was one year old.

So I wouldn't miss this graduation because Liza has long been dear to me. I also went to be with my sister on this very special occasion. The two of us had had quite a year. Our parents had both reached a point where they were finding it very hard to keep living on their own. Dad's advancing Alzheimer's disease was more than mom could cope with in her own frail and pain-filled state of health.

Together my sister and I worked the problem with mom. Together we tried to figure out what to do. Miraculously we found two excellent places for them to go where they could each get what they need. Both places were near my sister, near each other. Together we helped them consider and choose. We packed the boxes, followed the movers around the house, arranged both ends of the journey. We did all this trying to deal with their pain and our pain of the ending of an era that we had all greatly loved—the California era—and the end, after nearly fifty years, of their being able to live together.

So, as I sat at that graduation next to Peg, all we had been through with those we loved that year was much on our minds. With so many times of struggle, I was glad to be able to be there at this time of jubilation.

Unknown to any of us until we opened the program, Liza graduated summa cum laude with a special award of highest honors ever from the music department. My Mom and Dad could not be there, but I sat next to her other Grandmother and Grandfather, Jane and Willard Wirtz. He was the Secretary of Labor under Kennedy and Johnson. Liza is their first grandchild, the first girl in the family, as they had only sons. To feel the pride vibrate through both Peg and Mrs. Wirtz was a splendid thing.

The best moment for me, however, had come at the church service that morning. I sat next to Peg in the exquisite little Anglican chapel set on a green. The service was simple, but very moving. Liza and a group she founded sang the music. The final song was Scottish, from an album by Charles and Craig Reid called *Sunshine on Leith.* (Leith is a great seaport.)

It begins "My heart was broken . . ." Now that sounds, certainly, utterly trite. But in that immense year of breaking and transition for all of us, it merely spoke what we had known.

I wish you could have heard her sing the intricate harmony with her friends—stirring in us all the sorrow of hearts broken, but also the truth of how we can heal and save one another, of the cleansing of tears, of the unspeakable gratitude for our births.

Tears welled up in my eyes and Peg's. For her birth and my birth. For our beloved sister Mary Lee's birth. For Dad's birth and Mom's birth—without which there could never have been Liza's birth and Boo's birth. So much beauty and kindness and tears clearing blindness.

Those beautiful young people sat down, and the Anglican priest rose for the final prayer of thanksgiving to be spoken by all of us. Row on row of families had come to graduation, assortments of ages and generations, the genetic strain so clear in the shape of faces and color of hair. The sum total of the effort and glory of raising families was inscribed on those faces. No one gets this far without seasons of enormous dark and light.

The prayer, which I think might be from the Book of Common Prayer, was this:

> Accept, O Lord, our thanks and praise for all that you have done for us. We thank you for setting us at tasks which demand our best efforts (my sister and I looked at each other), and for leading us to accomplishments which satisfy and delight us. We thank you for those disappointments and failures that lead us to acknowledge our dependence on you alone.

This is only known to the dispossessed, I thought to myself. It is that dependence that is the mother of our truest hope.

He ended, "Grant us the gift of your Spirit, that we may know you and make you known, and through you and in all places, we may give thanks to you in all things. Amen."

The other incident I want to put a frame around happened that same year. It was somehow even more basic. It was at Christmas.

I stopped in Tennessee on my way home to Florida when our fall program ended. The endings of programs, I have learned since then, are hard. Saying good-bye to the superb people who come to us for sabbatical can be wrenching. I hit the road for the long drive just escaping a snowstorm.

I was spent and empty and sad when I reached my sister's. They waited with hugs and music and scotch and marvelous food. Two days later we had a gathering. Mom came from the retirement complex where she has an independent apartment but communal meals. We picked up dad from the family where he lives, an extraordinary mountain family who has kept Alzheimer's people in their home for years.

I hadn't seen him since October and I did not know what to expect. He did not seem to know me. Rationally you know that this is a probable progression of the disease. When it happens to you—your father does not know you, only knows you are someone he ought to know—it is very hard.

He was weak. He stared into space through much of the decorating of the tree and the exchange of presents. He warmed to the pie and ice cream. We all smiled, assured. This was the dad we knew. No one could surpass his love of sweets.

The time came quickly when we knew we needed to take him back. He was tiring and feeling confused by the intricacies of the celebration. He looked relieved when we asked if he wanted to go.

My sister and I left to take him home. He lives forty-five minutes away. I was driving, looking into the setting sun. I was afraid of a migraine, often light-triggered. But gradually the intensity mellowed, the world was filled with soft color. It outlined great bare trees and even gave a graciousness to telephone poles. The color caught in the Tennessee River beside us. Dad has always loved the sunset.

"Look, Dad, look."

"Uh, huh," he said. But we knew he really did not see.

From the back seat my sister, gently, fighting a profound sadness, began to sing Christmas carols. First a rousing one to keep our spirits up:

> Deck the halls with boughs of holly.
> Fa la la la la la la la la.

I thought of Arthur and Guinevere in Camelot in their great sorrow and conflictedness as they sang: "What do the simple folk do? Do you know? They sing . . . ."

She encouraged dad to sing. He smiled a little, but no sound came. She said "This is your favorite, Dad." And she began.

Then came his voice, that clear full true tenor we had heard all our lives, the voice that is in Liza's genes. It brought back a tidal wave of memories. We had heard it in ditties before six a.m. We had heard it doing dishes. We had heard it always on long trips, backing out of the driveway: "We're off to see the wizard, the wonderful wizard of Oz." It was a voice carrying so many layers of experience, tones, moods, nuances, all our lives long. And now he sang with her in that voice the carol he most loved, slowly, clearly:

> God rest ye merry gentlemen, let nothing ye dismay,
> Remember Christ our Savior was born on Christmas day.

This is our hope. This is the whole of it. Peace is not cool and blue. It is born of desolation. Dispossession. But it is born.

We are not alone. God is among us. Within us. Around us. Enfolding us. "All shall be well, and all shall be well, and all manner of thing shall be well."

In the strength of that hope for all of us gentlefolk, we pray:

> Grant us through your Spirit that we may know you and make you known, at all times and in all places, and give you thanks in all things. Amen.

10

The Hunger and the Feast

Life is a blending of opposites, polarities, paradoxes. In a single day, there is light and dark, waking and sleeping, resting and working, high tides and low. In every month the moon grows full until the pale and slender curve appears again. In every year the seasons follow one another. There is rhythm, alteration, variance.

The stages of our lives vary their demands. When we grow out of our dependence to autonomy, we must prepare to face dependence once again. In the course of days we all know embarrassment and glory, power and illness, loss and unexpected love.

I have come to see the main polarity in the currents of our soul as the hunger and the feast. What I call the hunger, Benedictine theologian Sebastian Moore describes in his book *The Inner Loneliness.* Moore writes about the universal loneliness that is at the heart of all of us; a tremendous yearning. He says it grows out of the core condition of the human being, which is self-awareness and self-love. What makes us unique of all creatures is that we can be aware of ourselves. We are even aware of that awareness. We can reflect on that awareness.

Now, at this moment, I can be aware of the chair beneath me at this desk. (Quite uncomfortable, in fact—too high, too deep, but too expensive to just throw out, and better than the kitchen chair I tried before!) I can be aware of the temperature on this muggy summer day, aware of a growing lessening of terror toward this new computer, aware of you, an imagined you, that might sometime be reading this. There is a rush of gladness as I think that may be so.

You may let yourself be conscious of where and how you are: your posture, your fatigue or restedness, the hand that holds the book, the tasks that you must still get done today, a sense, perhaps, of some response to me.

We are both letting ourselves be aware of our awareness. Doing that only intensifies what happens all the time. When we turn our focus to ourselves, we are familiar.

This self-awareness is a *being with* ourselves. The part of you or me that reflected on how comfortable we were, on how our day was going, that part *is being with* ourselves. Moore says that this being-with is our primary act of existing. It is also our primary motive for living. It is self-love, he says. "Self-awareness flowers as self-love."

When I first read that, I objected. (I often answer back or cheer agreement when I read. The margins of my books are filled with comments.) "I think you're wrong!" I wrote in yellow by that statement. What I meant is that I don't think self-love flowers very often. We can be cruel, remorseless, to ourselves. We can put everyone else's needs above our own. We can care about ourselves more poorly than anyone. But as I read on, I understood his meaning.

He explains that I can't help but feel myself as someone special. I am all there is in my own being. I can't escape being important to myself. I'm all I have inside of me. I know I am special because when I get hurt or put down or ignored, I feel pain and outrage. "Wait a minute! I matter!" I can't help crying out.

I had a vivid experience of that in Miami. I had gone to a college campus there to take a workshop from William

Glasser. It was superb and I was very glad I went. During the first break, I had to make a phone call. Nine people waited at the only booth. The break was only fifteen minutes, so I didn't think I would get to make my call. Across the street I had seen a library: perhaps it had a phone.

I walked up the steps and in the door and was looking around, when suddenly a shrill, loud voice called: "Miss! Miss! Where is your I.D.?"

"I don't have an I.D.," I answered.

"Then you do not belong in here. This is not open to the public. Get out of here right now!" The librarian looked eight feet tall to me, the sternest face I'd ever seen. She was pointing her long finger at the door. My face inflamed. Saying nothing, I followed her finger out the door.

Walking down the steps I felt the outrage Moore described. "Just wait a minute. You have no right to treat me that way. O.K., I broke the rule. I didn't mean to, I was just looking for a phone. Don't talk to me that way! I'm a person. I matter . . . ."

Self-love flows necessarily out of self-awareness. I can't escape being special to myself. And out of self-love there flows the fact that "I want this self that I love to be important to another." Experience testifies that there is no greater satisfaction than knowing you count in the eyes of someone special, that that person's life is different because of you, and happy because you are around.

> It is wrongly supposed that people want to be important to each other because they do not feel important in themselves. On the contrary, it is because individuals feel they are "special" that they want this specialness to make a difference to another.[1]

We all know what this is like. A time I am remembering happened with my younger sister's daughter, Claire. At the time she was about four. She was one of those children who look like they come from an enchanted place. She was tiny and delicate and graceful, with masses of dark curls and huge blue eyes. She looked like a fairy child. We were the only ones home, and she told me she wanted to introduce me to her "buddies." These were her stuffed animals and dolls. One by one she brought them in to show me. She told me each one's name, and when they had been born (Christmas, or her birthday, or just one day when mom had been in a great mood). She told me about the things they'd done, the times they had been good, the times she'd had to spank them. She pointed out the ones who never went to bed on time.

I was spellbound, afraid to speak, lest she would stop. I loved the afternoon. The next day I went home, and my sister called that night to tell me what had happened when I left. Claire was drawing. There were four figures, made with sticks and circles for the heads. The last one had a big circle with a smaller circle on each side. My sister asked her who they were. "This is you, Mommy, and this is Dad, and this is Sam (her older brother)."

"And who's this other person?"

"That is my new friend, Aunt Pat."

"Well, what are these things on Aunt Pat's head?"

"They're ears. Aunt Pat really listens. That makes me feel special."

Well. My heart beat with such delight, I knew she must be able to hear it through the phone. That this precious little one who was so dear to me, *cared* that I listened! I was transported. I mattered to her! I told my kids, I told the neighbors, I even stopped the mailman. I felt tremendously important.

Another instance of the joy of being special happened when Boo was small. He had the curved cheeks and rounded nose and pudgy hands of five-year-olds. His eyes were big and dark, and he had dimples. He had a shyness that was totally disarming. We were at a 4-H horse show, an all day event in which Kadee was competing with her pony, Princess. Boo had really wanted to go, but he began to feel tired and lost in the crowd by about ten a.m. A wonderful Cuban friend of mine, Evora, was running the show, and we went to talk to her. Her son, George, was there, a massive football-playing high school junior.

George took one look at Boo and squatted down level with him. "Getting tired, Ombre?" he asked. It was a joke that he called Boo the Ombre, or Frito Bandito, because Boo liked to wear a cowboy hat.

"Uh-huh," said Boo, awed that Big George was talking to him.

"Want to ride on my back?" George asked.

"Oh, *yeah*!" Boo answered.

The rest of the day Boo rode on George's back or shoulders. He was above everyone, seeing all there was to see, part of all that happened, but, best of all, close to George himself.

A couple of weeks later it was nearing Valentine's Day. Boo had a little packet of Valentines, twenty-five for sixty cents, I think they were then. He was naming to himself who would get which one. In the middle of this task he asked me if I thought George would think it was dumb if he sent him one. "I think he'd like it," I replied.

Valentine's Day night Evora called me. She told me George had had great piles of Valentines: a dozen girls had sent them, also aunts and cousins. He glanced at all of them. But the one that captured him was Boo's. He brought it in to show her, and went around all evening saying softly: "Boo sent me a Valentine. Boo really likes me!"

We need to be found special.

This hunger to be special matures in us. It becomes a great wish to give myself as I know myself most deeply to another, to be totally received and appreciated and loved and understood. To be one with the one whom I am made for. We all have this.

I read a lot of fiction. I get piles of books at the paperback exchange. Some of them are excellent, challenging and deepening. But many of them are what I call airplane reading: totally frivolous, requiring no concentration. Many of them are mysteries. Some are romances. If you've never read a romance, I must explain that the theme of every one is similar. Two people who have never been well loved by other people in their lives attract each other. You can tell the hero or heroine because they always have some unusual color eyes: amethyst or emerald, violet or periwinkle. The man is almost always handsome and powerful and rich, apparently arrogant, but vulnerable underneath. The woman is usually poor or helpless or in trouble, always beautiful, spirited, and resourceful. There are great convolutions of plot with misunderstandings and frustrations, but in the last two pages resolution and ecstatic union occur.

These books sell because at some level we all long for this. We want to be discovered under our facade; to be understood, cherished, and delighted in; to be known in our most hidden places, and to have everything that is known loved. We want someone who is "all there is to me;" someone who, like Kenny Rogers' song, *Lady*, "will come into my life and make me whole."

We cannot do this for each other. As Moore says, we are all limited by our own boundaries, our awarenesses. We cannot get inside, interior, to another. We cannot meet totally. We try sometimes, we try hard, but even in the best of these attempts we cannot sustain it completely. The French have a powerful saying—"After the loving, the sadness." The best of our moments of union are followed by the awareness of the other as separate. And if we expect the other to complete us forever, we can only be frustrated. Expecting that of the other dooms the relationship. There is one who can complete us, one who can be experienced as totally inward, knowing us from within as no one else can. There is one who has no limits, no boundaries, who is all there is to me. One whom I am made for. And this, Thomas Aquinas would say, is the one we call God.[2]

Every one of us is created with the hunger for the Other. This ineluctable loneliness is the core of being human. "That desire that is central to my being and living, and that no other human can satisfy, *is not in vain,* does not come from nowhere."[3] It is created in us by the one who has to love, who is love, whose whole being is that mysterious Other that we meet in answer to that universal longing.[4]

This is a very, very important truth. The amazing thing is how little it operates in the awareness of most of us. All of us have this loneliness. For some it is never made conscious. They experience it as a kind of restlessness, a discontent with life, a haunting sense of "Is this all there is?"[5]

For others there is awareness of the loneliness, but it is focused on the search for the other, for the perfect match, for the woman of my dreams, or the man for me. At fifteen, Kadee said to me one day, "I know he's out there, Mama, my dream man. I know he'll find me." (In the next seven years, many different potential dream men pulled their cars up in our driveway. When she was twenty-two, she said to me one day: "You know, Mom, there is no dream man. Relationships are hard. They take work. You just feel more like working on them with some people than others.")

In my work with groups of separated and divorced around the country many people have said to me "I must find him . . . I must find her . . . I have so much to give, I want a chance to give it. I want to find a person I can be happy with."

This is just what Moore is saying. We want to be special to someone. We want to make them happy with our specialness. This is a wonderful thing when it happens, if it happens. But it does not take away, after a while, the loneliness, the hunger. We cannot escape it. In the best of marriages it will be there. We cannot *complete* each other. If we understand that, we are really freed to love while acknowledging the larger longing.

We perhaps all feel the pull of it sometimes when we look at the night sky. Moore says: "In me the galaxies hunger for God."[6] I am convinced that all the time we hunger, all the time we yearn, all the time we search and reach out and want and turn upon our pillow hoping sleep might soothe that wanting, there is at the heart of us the one who says: "Before the day star, I called you by name."

I don't know anything more important than that.

A few years ago I was traveling to the Far East to do a series of workshops for Air Force chaplains. On my flight from Los Angeles to Hawaii I was seated next to a handsome Korean man in his sixties. (If you have seen any of the *Karate Kid* films, he looked very much like Mr. Miyagi.) It was a very long flight, we talked for hours. He had an engaging way of speaking, a combination of dignified, orientally musical phrases interspersed with completely outdated American slang. It was charming. For example, he asked me what I was travelling to do. I told him it was a tour for Air Force chaplains. He asked what I was speaking on. I told him spirituality.

"Ah so," he said, "you, a young woman, are travelling thousands of miles to talk to men of God about God. Is that right?"

"Well, yes, I guess it is."

"How you like dem apples?" he exclaimed and laughed and laughed.

We talked about many things, about births and deaths, about achievements and endings, about surprises and losses. About dealing with it all. At one point we prayed together, in silence, for about twenty minutes.

As we began the final descent he said something with a twinkle in his eyes. "At the end of this extraordinary journey I feel as if I should pass on to you the secret of life."

"You do?"

"But I can't pass it on."

"Why not?" I asked, almost afraid to learn why.

"Because you already know it."

"I do?"

"You just don't entirely know you know it yet."

"What do I know that I don't know I know?" I asked slowly.

"That the hunger is a *good* thing," he replied.

It took me about two years to figure that out. I was teaching for a week in summer school at Fordham University in New York. It was the first time I met Michael Himes, who was teaching that same week. His classes were in the morning, and I went to them all. At one point he spoke about hunger. He said when he was in the seminary they used to call it "Himes' doughnut hole theory."

"There is," he said, "an emptiness at the heart of every human. The very essence of being finite is that the emptiness is there. It is made for the infinite to fill. And the infinite, God, the one who is least inadequately defined as purely other-directed love, is dying to fill us. Dying to fill us."

I sat in that classroom, and I heard again the voice of the man on the plane to the Orient. I knew that the hunger he had spoken of was the same as Himes was describing. I know now it is the same as Moore's ineluctable loneliness. It is behind the search for the perfect match, and the search for the holy grail. It is Augustine's restlessness for the beauty, ever ancient, ever new.

We needn't be afraid of the hunger. It is, as my friend said on the plane, a good thing. If we can accept it, it is a good thing. It is the glory of being human, for it is made for God's great love. And God is dying to fill it; moving mountains to fill it; leading us into green pastures to fill it; sending messengers into the hedgerows and the byroads to fill it. God is waiting, never losing hope, outside every barrier we have, wanting more than anything to fill it.

Blessed are we who hunger, for we will be filled by God.

A corollary to this, a polarity, another part of the learning is that all life is a balance. There is always "on the other hand."

As hard as it is to accept and embrace the hunger, for many of us it becomes even harder to accept its inevitable polarity, even harder to say "yes" to the feast. Yet the image of the banquet is as old as the truth of the hunger.

There are possible reasons. Moore suggests the first. He says there is a deep perversity in all of us, "a deep distrust of happiness, of free unconditional joy in the human mind. There is a certain natural pessimism, parsimony, puritanism, about the way we think of ourselves."[7] This is an ancient mind set.

I think there is another reason, too. I think when we learn to live with the hunger, we get afraid we will forget how to do it if we go to the feast. I have found this true in people who have suffered some great loss.

I knew a man once who had been a prisoner of the Vietnamese for five and a half years. His helicopter was shot down in the early part of that war. His wife was a friend, a fascinating woman who had moved to our town in central Florida because her research had shown it had the climate most like Vietnam in all the country. If he were released in winter, she did not want him to have to adjust to the bitter cold of their home state.

A few weeks after his release they came to dinner. It was his first venture out of the privacy of his family. Six of us gathered for a picnic in the barn. The other four had gone walking in the blooming orange grove, but he had stayed behind with me as I was putting out the food. I glanced at him, and saw a look like fear upon his face.

"What is it, Ken?" I asked.

"I'm afraid of your food."

"Have you been talking to my kids?" I asked, attempting to be light.

He shook his head. Then slowly he began to speak: "For five years I learned how to live on rotten fish heads and dirty rice. I learned how to feed myself from within. And now when I can eat again, I am afraid. I look at your food, that chicken and barbecued ribs and salad and biscuits and chocolate cake and pecan pie, all that loving food. And I feel fear. What happens if I get used to the food? What happens if I get used to the love? And then one day I wake up and I am back again in a bamboo cage, trying to scrape the rice off the muddy ground, trying not to retch on the rotten fish. What if I forget how to feed myself from within?"

We can get afraid when we have made friends with the hunger, afraid to take the gift of the feast.

I was challenged on being closed to the feast one fall in New York City. I had been asked to speak at the cathedral in Brooklyn in a series called "Women as Prophetic Witnesses." I had spoken, and was at the reception in the cathedral rectory when a man came up to me. He was powerfully built, gray-bearded, dressed in navy blue. His eyes were piercing, and he was rather daunting until he grinned. He asked me how long I was going to be in New York. I told him I was leaving the day after tomorrow. He asked what I was going to do with my day in New York.

"Well, from here I'm going on to Rochester where I have to give a talk. I'm going to work on what I need to say."

His eyes narrowed and intensified. "What? You are going to stay in and work on a talk? Maybe you don't understand. This is not Des Moines or Hackensack. You are in The City. There are museums and music and shows and shops; people of every sound and color; the finest food on the continent. You could watch the sun set from the top of the World Trade Building. And you think you'll stay in and work on a talk?"

"Look, lady," he continued, "do you think there is an unlimited number of days out there just waiting for you to get caught up on your work? Do you think the gold ring is on the merry-go-round to decorate the rim of the sky? It's there to reach for. Go for it."

I went for it. I called a friend, a woman religious who lived near, and she put aside what she was doing, and we took on New York. We looked at the wonders of texture, shape, and color at the Metropolitan Museum of Art. We had lunch in a tavern sitting in a booth that had a plaque that said: "In this booth, O. Henry wrote in one afternoon *The Gift of the Magi*." We went to Tiffany's and pretended we were rich. We tried on rings and held up crystal to the light.

We waited in line for half-price theater tickets in Times Square. A great thing happened. The wait took forty minutes, so we got some sense of who was near us in the line. When the woman in front of us stepped up to buy six tickets, she realized that she was three dollars short of what she needed. She was distraught. The ticket seller said: "Eitha pay da money or get outta da way."

She was counting change, but it was plain to me she couldn't make the total. I pulled three singles out to hand to her. "Here take this," I said to her. A gasp went through the waiting crowd. If I had mugged her they wouldn't have been as shocked.

"Oh, I couldn't," she replied. "How could I be this dumb? I knew how much these tickets were. I can't believe I did this!"

"Take the money," I said again. "What's three dollars in New York? A cup of coffee? Take it."

"I can't," she said. "Well, maybe I could meet you somewhere at a certain time and pay you back."

"Look, lady," I said. "Do you think there is an unlimited number of offers like this just waiting for you to get around to taking it? Do you think the gold ring is on the merry-go-round to decorate the rim of the sky? It's there to reach for! Go for it!"

She laughed and took the money.

My friend and I ended up that day at the top of the World Trade Building at sunset. I will never forget it. Blazing color catching all there was on fire: the river and the sky and all the windows of Manhattan. Way down below there was Liberty holding her torch. She was in the scaffolding like a lace dress. Below her was Ellis Island where my great-grandparents had come from Ireland so their children, and their children's children, and their children, could have life. There I was looking down on it in the sunset.

I could have missed it. It was there for me. We can miss so much that is there for us all. Love meets us in the loneliness, transforming it into belonging. Love gives us the hunger as a call to the feast; Love who is the author of sunsets and liberty and each of our bright and splendid specialness.

We cannot often get to a feast like the top of the World Trade Building, but there are lots of kinds of feasts for the claiming. It is like our opening the doors on beauty, truth, and goodness that take us into hope.

We could plan a phone conversation at sunset, each looking out our windows. We could buy tulips for a purple vase. We could drink Grand Marnier in a stemmed glass filled with ice. We could have a deep bath, or sleep an extra hour, or heat milk for café au lait. We could pick blueberries in early morning with our children or try to throw a boomerang or sing the harmony of barbershop quartet. We could exchange listening with a friend while walking in an evening. We could bring a surprise to someone who least expects it, and then have a share because the breaking open of the bounty with another is the heart of being graced. There are a thousand ways to come around the banquet table.

Blessed are we who know the hunger *and* the feast. For we have the cross *and* the empty tomb. And that is the gold ring.

11

Each Day a Grace

I come to the end of this book as I come to the end of the summer. It has been a golden time, a time of rest and long, free days. I have not been in a hurry once since I came home. I have almost never put on stockings, and most of every day gone barefoot. I have not set an alarm to wake me any morning. I have seen the best of fireworks, and had a birthday dinner cooked and served with fanfare by my children.

I dusted off my tennis racket and swam in the warm waters of the lake. I made biscuits for my family and gave myself over to a rainfall. I re-read Tolkien's *Lord of the Rings*, reacquainting myself with Frodo and Gandalf the Wizard, with the elf-queen Galadriel and Aragorn of Arathorn, the healer-king. I sat around a table seven hours of an afternoon and evening with my closest friends here, come from all directions. I've learned the shapes and names and calls of birds that live around my house, taught by my daughter Kadee.

Mother Mouton would say it has been *la Delicatesse du Bon Dieu*. Each day has been a grace. When I left Notre Dame, I had no idea this was what the summer held. I had turned down speaking engagements to try to write this book, and to brave the total strangeness of the computer-realm to make it happen. I planned it before I knew that all my children would be home, that we could have these weeks to meet together. It has been the kind of leisure I longed for in that winter when I tried to warm the brandy.

The thread through all the days has been this writing. I have tried to picture you, you who are now reading, you in your place on the moving walkway, your room on this earth, you in the mixedness of your life, you with all your experiences of "life is hard, but life is good."

I know in your life, as John Shea says in *The God Who Fell From Heaven,* "Mystery is on the initiative." God is on the move, expressed by St. John as "God *first* loves us." I wish I could hear your songs and stories, the things that make you laugh. I wish I knew what gives you hope. Perhaps someday you'll pass it on to me.

I want to say to you, "Keep your eyes open! Eggs might be half-price today." I want to call after you on a jetway: "Look for the surprises." I want to say to you, from under a baseball cap, "Life is not fair. But sometimes we get incredible breaks in our favor."

I want to tell you, descending into Hawaii: "This is the secret of life: the hunger is a good thing."

"But, on the other hand, go for the gold ring."

I leave you with a story. This winter was the Gulf War. In the ageless desert under the same stars that shone their cold clear light on Israelites and Babylonians, my son Randy pitched a tent.

Those were terrible days for me, watching the television accounts minute by minute. What madness. My fear seemed like an ancient thing. All mothers with their children gone to war must have felt this fear forever.

Twenty-five years before, I was waiting for Randy to be born. It was eleven months after his brother, my first son, was stillborn at full term. I was waiting, hoping, praying he would be born safely. All these years later I was waiting, hoping, praying for a different kind of safe delivery. Thinking of him through all the days and nights. And all the other sons and daughters of other mothers under that same sky.

I thought of Frodo, Tolkien's improbable hero-hobbit, saying to Sam Gamgee, trying to figure out the very strange happenings they found themselves in the middle of: "What story are we in?"

"What story is *this*?" I asked myself, looking out into the night.

I told myself, "Randy was born smiling. Don't forget that. Smiling. He comes to this power and confusion with the strong home run humor of his soul. He feels the angst of this strange desert war, he is tired and wet and cold and hot and dry and hungry and cranky and bored and scared and bewildered and excited and deep in prayer. He feels it. He wonders. He gets pumped up. He falls asleep beside his truck. In all of this he has a merry sense of self. A kind of rudimentary courage. He can be both strong and merciful."

It is in this summer, this golden time, this unhurried encounter with time for conversations, that I heard the story.

His unit was deep in Iraq, past the Euphrates River, far into the territory of the oldest stories of our scriptures. They were behind the Republican Guard. He had his weapon, a Stinger missile, a hand-held trajectile to shoot down planes. He was with a partner in this war's jeep, the humvee. His partner, by some fluke, was also a Floridian, a Cuban. Randy's roots here go back five generations. This friend had just arrived. But they had Florida in common and were grateful for the bond.

The battle was the fiercest contest of the war. It had been predicted to be "the mother of all battles." But Randy said it was eclipsed that night by a mammoth thunderstorm, the most spectacular of his whole life experience. (We have in this area of central Florida the worst storms in the continental U.S. He *knows* storms.) After the battle on earth and heaven, violently erupting, exploding, conflagrating, there was a silence. "This is my birthday," he said to himself. "And somehow I'm still alive."

In the days that followed the battle there were Iraqi troop surrenders. In our conversation he described them to me, the scar from going through the sliding glass door pale upon his desert-darkened face. "Mom, some of them were deaf or blinded. They didn't have helmets. Hell, they didn't even have shoes. When I approached them, I'd have to keep talking, talking as gently as I could. Trying to communicate with my tone of voice that I would not hurt them. I offered them water, liters of water, and they would not stop drinking until every drop was gone. I offered them food, and they bit through the plastic wrappings."

It's hard to write this, I feel it so intensely. I don't know what I was more afraid of, that Randy would be killed in that desert, or that he would have to kill. I was wracked with the horror of that. I would wake up filled with dread, thinking of him killing someone, or falling dead himself.

The truth was, he never fired his weapon. There were no planes, nothing for a Stinger to destroy. Instead of giving death, instead of wielding harm, he offered food and drink. He was able to offer mercy. Mercy is the strongest sign of God.

"Well," my grandfather would say, "think of that."

We pass on the stories to each other, the stories that contain the central truths of life. Many years ago, driving one hundred miles each way to graduate school, I learned Shakespeare's telling of Agincourt by the dashboard light. What moved me most as I would recite it aloud was that, as a story to rally courage against all odds, it had been passed on. The ones returning from the battle told it to their loved ones, to their neighbors, to their friends, and ever after that to children when they were old enough to hear. As I struggled with my life I felt the story passed along to me.

In the human family we pass the stories on. Details get blurred, new ones get added on, some aspects change. The tale itself is alive. The basic truth remains that made the story worth the telling.

My mother recounts what happened to her great-grandmother when she first came to America. She had sailed with her father from Ireland, the ship landing in Boston. All the money the family had been able to save to give them a start was in coins sewed inside his vest. He left his daughter in Boston to go to Philadelphia where a relative might have work for him. When he got there an epidemic was ravaging the poor. He sickened with the plague, and died, buried in some unmarked place still wearing the vest.

Against all odds. My mother's great-grandmother was left penniless, alone. Somehow she made her way using the skill she'd learned in Ireland of making lace. A Quaker doctor's family took her in, and she married a young man apprenticed to the doctor. "Otherwise I would not be here telling you this story," my mother would say with her little understated smile.

Women tell the story. Men returning after Agincourt. Israelites in the desert. Christians after Pentecost. In the human family mystery is experienced in life. The tales are told of mixedness, of suffering and mercy, of the hungers and the feasts. Men and women, generation after generation, pass the stories on, and in the telling, faith and hope and love are nurtured. Embodied in the stories are the lessons of the heart.

Notes

2: *Life Is Mixed*

[1] Madeleine L'Engle, *A Circle of Quiet, Crosswicks Journal Book I* (San Francisco: Harper and Row, 1972), p. 154.

[2] For a delightful modern fairy tale on this theme, read *Princess Bride* by William Goldman (New York: Harcourt Brace Jovanovich, 1973).

4: *Spirituality Is* Not *Removed From Life*

[1] Gabriel Moran, *Theology of Revelation* (New York: Herder and Herder, 1966), p. 50.

5: *Sacrament Is God Revealed in Life*

[1] Michael Downey, *Clothed in Christ* (New York: Crossroads, 1987), pp. 33-34.

[2] Alice Walker, *The Color Purple* (New York: Washington Square Press, 1982), p. 178.

[3] Annie Dillard, *Pilgrim at Tinker Creek* (New York: Harper's Magazine Press, 1974), p. 9.

[4] Kathleen D. Chesto, "Echoes of the Passion," *Praying*, March/April 1991, p. 13.

6: *Mercy Is God's Clearest Sign*

[1] Matthew Fox, *Meditations With Meister Eckhart* (Sante Fe, NM: Bear and Co., 1982), p. 111.

[2] Thomas Merton, *The Complete Poems of Thomas Merton* (New York: New Direction Publishing Corp., 1977), p. 366. For a beautiful reading of this poem in the Gethsemani Abbey see "A Companion to Prayer" audiocassette by the Notre Dame Folk Choir and the Monastic Schola of Gethsemani (Ave Maria Press).

[3] J. R. R. Tolkien, *The Return of the King* (New York: Ballantine Books, 1989), p. 283.

7: *Forgiveness Interweaves With Mercy*

[1] An excellent book on the process of forgiving is *Learning to Forgive* by Doris Donnelly (New York: Macmillan Publishing Co., 1979).

8: *Suffering Can Lead to Life*

[1] For a full treatment of this idea, see Demetrius Dumm's excellent book, *Flowers in the Desert* (New York: Paulist Press, 1987).

[2] Elizabeth Goudge, *The Heart of the Family* (New York: Coward-McCann, Inc., 1953), p. 129.

[3] From *The Poetry of Robert Frost* edited Edward Connery Lathem. Copyright 1923, © 1969 by Holt, Rinehart and Winston. Copyright 1951 by Robert Frost. Reprinted by permission of Henry Holt and Company, Inc.

10: *The Hunger and the Feast*

[1] Sebastian Moore, *The Inner Loneliness* (New York: Crossroads, 1982), p. 11.

[2] See p. 12.

[3] See p. 14.

[4] See p. 12.

[5] See p. 14.

[6] See p. 104.

[7] See p. 24.